DON MIGUEL RUIZ'S

LITTLE BOOK
OF WISDOM

DON MIGUEL RUIZ'S
LITTLE BOOK
OF WISDOM

The Essential Teachings

DON MIGUEL RUIZ JR.

Hierophant publishing

Cover design by Emma Smith
Cover art by Nicholas Wilton
Interior Design by Frame25 Productions

Hierophant Publishing
8301 Broadway, Suite 219
San Antonio, TX 78209
888-800-4240
www.hierophantpublishing.com

If you are unable to order this book from your local bookseller,
you may order directly from the publisher.

Library of Congress Control Number: 2016963704

ISBN 978-1-938289-60-6
10 9 8 7 6 5 4 3

For my children, so they may always have access to their grandfather's wisdom.

For you, father. I hope you find this collection of stories and sayings a worthy embodiment of the legacy you have left to the world.

And to everyone I love.

Table of Contents

Introduction

When my daughter Audrey was seven years old, I took her to our local bookstore to buy a new bedtime storybook. As we were walking over to the children's section, I noticed my father's book, *The Four Agreements* (Amber-Allen Publishing, 1997), displayed prominently on the shelf marked "Staff Favorites."

I smiled and looked at it with great pride and joy, and marveled at how it still resonates with people so many years after the book was first released. I remember looking for it in bookstores when it first came out, and no bookstore would carry it. I looked for it for several months at different stores, and I always came up empty. It seems funny now, but in those days I wondered if I would ever see it on a bookshelf on the sales floor—there for everyone to see.

About a year after it was published, I found it for the first time in a bookstore in Berkeley, California. I was so overjoyed that I couldn't stop smiling for several hours;

the feeling of seeing my father's first book on the shelf was such a moment of happiness for me. Unlike all the books I had ever purchased, this one came from the wisdom of my family's tradition, in my father's own words, and now the world could read it.

Marveling at the journey my father had made over the last several years, I turned to Audrey and said, "Honey, if there is ever a time when you need advice or want to connect with your grandpa, and he is too far away to be reached, you can always come to a bookstore or library and find him. In the pages of his books he will share with you what he knows about love and life; his voice is here to help you." It felt wonderful to be able to say that, because the oral tradition that our family has been sharing through so many generations is still alive, and it is here for anyone who wants to find help, including my own children.

At the same time, I knew there was more to my father's wisdom than he had been able to include in his existing books. I dreamed at that moment that one day such a book would exist: one that contained this additional wisdom. I am pleased to say that the book you are currently holding in your hands has been manifested through this intention.

My father's wisdom, which he began teaching in the mid 1980s, springs from our family's Toltec tradition.

The Toltecs were a group of Native Americans that came together in south central Mexico 2,500 years ago. They are the builders of the pyramids in Teotihuacan, Mexico. The word *Toltec* is a Nahuatl word that means "artist," as the Toltecs believed every human being was the artist of his or her own life. My family's Toltec wisdom has been handed down from generation to generation, sometimes in secrecy when the politics of the day required it. My father learned our tradition from his mother, Madre Sarita, and from his grandfather, don Leonardo.

What many people do not know is that earlier in his life, my father was not very interested in the traditional wisdom of my family. His passion was medicine, and he attended medical school and became a physician. Shortly after graduating from medical school, however, he had a near-death experience that was to change him greatly. (I have included his first-person account of this event at the start of this book.)

It was after this near-death experience that he became interested in our family's wisdom tradition, and he began an apprenticeship to Madre Sarita. At first, he was only able to study every weekend in San Diego, California, while also maintaining his medical practice in Tijuana, Mexico. As he grew more knowledgeable about our family's wisdom, his training in Western science and psychology allowed him to see these teachings in a new way. Consequently, he synthesized the two traditions and was able to develop ways to communicate his teachings in a language that could resonate in the modern world.

As his oldest son, I remember well his journey from Dr. Miguel Ruiz to the master teacher and author don Miguel Ruiz. I remember when he let my mother know that he was leaving medicine altogether in pursuit of his passion, and felt the financial consequence his decision had for our family. I remember the humble beginnings of his first classes, when only four or five people would attend. Looking back, I see the full line of his evolution as a teacher, beginning with the practice of sharing the tradition with students and continuing by always searching for the best means by which each student could resonate with a lesson. Through this resonance, he knew his students could attain a moment of clarity. As his teaching continued, he began to let go of the old Toltec symbols in our family's oral tradition. In their place, he developed a language that he would simply call "common sense."

My father's lessons have helped so many people find their authentic selves, heal from the wounds that domestication has left in their lives, and live a life imbued with unconditional love. Those who have followed his teachings have been able to harmoniously create their own personal dream.

And this brings me back to the goal and purpose of this book. I want to do my best to record as much of my father's legacy of wisdom as I can in these pages. I have collected here my father's most essential teachings, taken from transcriptions of lectures, presentations, and interviews, as well as from private moments in which he shared his wisdom with my brothers and myself.

Not surprisingly, it is these private moments that have impacted me the most—when my father would teach us without so many words, but rather through example. With this in mind, I have included a collection of anecdotal stories in the final part of this book, describing some of these moments.

The bulk of this book forms what I call the Wisdom Passages. These are the essential teachings, and as you read these passages, I would like to make a few suggestions to help you get the most out of the wisdom they contain.

Listen with your heart

As you read the wisdom passages, your mind may want to take over, working hard to understand my father's words, but remember: he is speaking to your *heart*. Allow his words to travel beyond your thinking mind (with all its acquired knowledge) and find their way into your beautiful heart. Only in your heart can you make room for this wisdom in a way that will allow transformation to take place.

Take your time

If you read more than two to three passages in a day, it may dilute the impact of the teachings. Even reading only one passage a day is a wonderful way to approach them. Give each one time to blossom in your heart.

Let the wisdom choose you

While you may certainly read the passages in the order they appear, another option is to pick up the book when you find yourself in a moment of difficulty or when faced with a decision. Turning to a random page, you may find a message that will inspire you about what to do next.

Lastly, for those of you who are not familiar with my father's previous books, you may want to begin by reading the opening story in Part 3, where I describe my own apprenticeship in the Toltec agreements. This will give you a basis for understanding some of the concepts and language in the wisdom passages section.

Now, let us begin *Don Miguel Ruiz's Little Book of Wisdom*.

Explanation of Key Terms

Agreements: Personal contracts we make with ourselves about the nature of reality and how we should behave in the world. Some agreements can help us create a beautiful life; others are responsible for drama and suffering.

Ally: The mind when it's acting on behalf of the human.

Attachment: An emotional or energetic investment. You can attach to external objects, beliefs, ideas, and even roles you play in the world.

Authentic Self: The Divine inside of you; the force that gives life to your mind and your body. It's similar to the concept of the spirit or the soul that is present in many religious traditions, but it's not exactly the same.

Awareness: Seeing things as they really are rather than through the filter of your knowledge.

Domestication: The system of teaching a human how to be a human according to a person's society or culture. We are domesticated when we adopt the beliefs and behaviors that others find acceptable.

Dream of the Planet: The way humanity perceives reality.

Faith: Believing in something without a doubt.

Four Agreements: Tools that an artist can use to create a new life, as found in the book *The Four Agreements* (Amber-Allen Publishing, 1997):

1. Be impeccable with your word.

2. Don't take anything personally.

3. Don't make assumptions.

4. Always do your best.

Knowledge: The many ideas and beliefs about reality that fill your mind in the form of words and symbols (language).

Mitote: A Nahuatl word that means chaos, and references the idea that it's as if a thousand people are talking in your mind simultaneously.

The Narrator: The voice in your head that is telling a story about what you are experiencing throughout the day. The narrator is the mind talking to itself.

Parasite: The mind when it is feeding off the emotional energy of the human.

Personal Dream: It's the unique way each individual interprets reality; his or her personal perspective.

Teotihuacan: An ancient city in south central Mexico that was the home of the Toltec people 2,500 years ago, well known for its pyramids.

Toltec people: An ancient group of Native Americans who came together in south and central Mexico to study perception. The word *Toltec* means "artist."

Toltec warrior: One who is committed to using the teachings of the Toltec tradition to win the inner battle over knowledge.

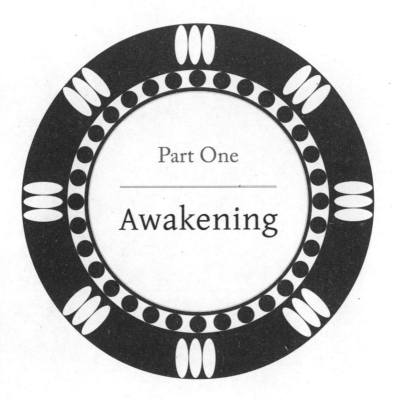

Part One

Awakening

Here is my father's own account of his near-death experience and the realizations that followed.

The story of Miguel Ruiz changed dramatically for me in one night, when I was a young medical student. This particular night, I made the same mistake that many young people do. I drank too much at a party, and afterwards I decided to drive back to Mexico City. This was, of course, a very bad decision. Not surprisingly, I fell asleep at the wheel and I hit a concrete wall. The car was totaled and my body was unconscious, but unhurt.

Now what is incredible is that when this happened, I saw the whole accident as though it was in slow motion. I saw my own body, unconscious at the wheel, and I knew my brain was unconscious as well. I saw that the car was totaled, but my body was completely safe. At that moment, I knew: *I am not my physical body*. Before then, I had heard so many times from my mother and grandfather that I wasn't my physical body, and of course I believed them, but from then on it was no longer a theory—for me it was a fact. That changed the course of my life completely, because this experience created a desire to learn even more.

After the near-death experience in the car crash, my whole personality changed. The way I perceived life was completely different: before the accident I thought everything was so important, and after the accident I could see everything I thought was important before—school, work, etc.—was completely irrelevant. I became consumed with one question: *what am I?* After the accident, I knew I wasn't this physical body; it was obvious. And it was obvious that I was not my identity either—Miguel the soccer player, or doctor, or husband, or whatever. Suddenly, since I was not what I believed I was prior to the accident, I realized I didn't know what I was. That really scared the knowledge in my mind. I know that many other people have had the same kind of experience, but some have denied it to themselves, and they just let it go and they adapt to life. They let knowledge take back over. I went in exactly the opposite direction; I really wanted to know who and what I am.

So I went deeper into the Toltec training of my family's tradition, and I was guided by my mother, my father, and my grandfather. It wasn't long before I had another profound experience.

It was in the summer, at around midnight, and I was in the desert. It was so hot that night that I couldn't sleep, so I decided to just walk around the desert. The moon was full, and as I gazed up at the sky, I had an experience that changed my understanding of everything yet again.

In that moment, I turned my face to the sky and I saw all those millions of stars. Without words, without thought, I knew that the light I was perceiving from all those stars, it came to me from millions of light-years away, and that all those stars were shining from different distances, but I was perceiving all those stars at the same time.

In that moment, I knew that some of those stars probably didn't even exist anymore. Maybe they had stopped existing thousands of years ago, or even millions of years ago, but I perceived everything in that single, present moment. It was so obvious to me then that everything I perceive is simply light coming from all the different directions to a place that seems like it is right behind my eyes and just between my ears, a place that represents only one point of view.

I also knew without a doubt that in the same way that I perceive the stars, the stars always perceive me. It was at this moment that I understood there is only One being that truly exists, and that being is alive. I saw my own body and I understood without a doubt that my body is a whole universe, it is complete in and of itself. Further, as I looked at my hands, I knew that every single cell of my body is also a whole universe. I looked around and saw the beautiful desert, and, without a doubt, I knew that the earth is a living organism and that I am a part of this Planet Earth. I understood also that all of the humans, all of us collectively, we are only one living being.

In this way, humanity is one organ of this beautiful Planet Earth. The oceans are another organ, the forests are another organ, all species taken together are yet another organ. We all work together for the benefit of this Planet Earth. Of course, at that time, I couldn't have put this into words; I just knew, and it's difficult to explain it even now. Please remember that the words I am using only point to the truth, as what I experienced cannot be fully explained with words.

That night in the desert, when I perceived all of this, I felt so much gratitude that it was overwhelming. That gratitude turned into generosity from that moment on, as my purpose became what it is today—to share the experience wherever I go and to let everybody know that life is so simple, so easy, but we make it very complicated. We complicate everything, and if we look at the story of humanity, we can see how we complicate things through violence, injustice, war, and more. You know this part of the story, of course.

In that moment of awakening, I knew that love is nothing but a perfect balance between gratitude and generosity. I also knew I had to make a choice, because I could deny the experience and forget about it, or I could embrace it and really share it with my own kind, with all of you. I knew in that moment that real love is completely unconditional. That realization changed my life completely.

I also understood that I am an artist, that every single human who lives on this Planet Earth is an artist, and that I was perceiving a masterpiece of art. The entire universe is a masterpiece of art, and as I was perceiving it, I was also recreating everything in my own brain.

What we call knowledge is simply the result of this perception we all have and our efforts to make sense of it to one another. In that moment, I understood that through my unique perception I create my own reality, my own world, my own universe. Of course I also understood right away that every single human around me does exactly the same thing, with or without awareness that it is happening. Each person creates their own reality, using the word as the instrument to create a story about that reality and themselves. That is why, for me, the impeccability of the word is the most important agreement that we can have with ourselves and with everybody around us, because it creates a world. Like me, everybody is an artist. Whatever I perceive is beautiful. Without a doubt, I know that perfection is the only state possible in existence. We humans, with or without our awareness of this fact, are perfect just the way we are.

Part Two

Wisdom
Passages

I come to you asking for a favor, and that favor is to help me to change the world. I'm not referring to the world of humanity, not the one "out there." I mean the world that you create in your own mind—the world that is only true for you and not for anyone else. You see, you create the story of your life. You create an entire reality that is only true for you. There are seven billion people in the world, all who create their own story. I create my personal world, but it is just a story. It's not real, and it's not true. In that same way, your story is not true either. The difference is that you believe it is true, and I do not. You begin to change your world the moment you realize it is not true, it is only a story.

Do you like the way you are living your life? Or, put another way, are you happy? If you are not happy, and you don't like the way you are living your life, then your first job is to find out why. Instead of blaming anyone else for this, start by finding out what you believe about yourself. Find out what you learned about yourself from your parents, your friends, and your teachers—not to blame any of them, no, but just to see if it helps you understand why you don't like the way you are living your life. Are you trying to live up to an image in your mind that was created by someone else? I mean, of course you created it, but whose standards did you use?

You are good enough—you are perfect—just the way you are. The goal of all this work is to love yourself exactly as you are, and to live your life the way you want to live it. That is what will make you happy.

Whatever we think we know is only an agreement, and it is based on our language. It's just words. If we call something a tree in our language, it is only true because we agree with the meaning of the symbol, not because it is really true. We have no idea what that thing is really, we just call it a tree. That's why I say we're all artists, and what we create is a whole story about ourselves and our world, and it's just a story. This story is only true because we narrate it with the language that we learn. It takes awareness to see beyond the stories we have created.

The Toltec teachings are the introduction to a new way of life that I call the way of the artist. In my own case, I became a medical doctor, a surgeon, and then I decided to change, to shift. That is what an artist does, and we are all artists—whether we realize it or not. In my own case, I wanted to leave the practice of medicine and go further into the human mind to really understand why humanity is the way it is.

What I found is that we create a story about ourselves through the way we perceive life and everything around us. We use the word in order to create the story that we live. We learn language, and our parents and others hook our attention, they download into our brain what they know. Then we go to school and the teachers do exactly the same thing. In this way, we learn to communicate with everyone around us. We use language in order to create everything that we believe—our whole story. It's really very simple when you see it, but the realization of it will change your life.

When you were born, you believed what you were taught without question. You accepted the identity and the roles that your parents gave you—this is your name, this is your home, and this is what we believe about life, and God, and more. They told you who you are, and before long, you were answering to the name they gave you, and by believing them you became like them. That isn't good or bad, it is simply the way it is. When you become aware, you realize that they don't know who you are, because they don't know who they are. Nobody does.

We don't need to know who we are in order to exist and be happy.

Knowledge presents the biggest challenge to personal freedom, because knowledge creates the image that you have of yourself. To conquer knowledge means to take away little by little every piece of the definition that you have built for yourself. This is so scary for most people, and many feel they cannot do it, because without knowledge to cling to the mind feels like it will die, or end up in a psychiatric institution. But when you let go of all those things you think you know about yourself, of all your images, you find freedom.

One of the most important things I do is to try and help people change their point of view. For instance, instead of focusing on all the drama that you have created in the past, or becoming over-whelmed by all the events that have happened in your life that you suffered over, you can put your attention on what you like and it will grow. It's your choice. In your mind you can have millions of ideas, but the work of the artist is to take action on those ideas, because you know that you have in your mind the power to make it real. That's why, in the Toltec tradition, the concept of dreaming is so important. The Toltecs know that dreaming is the first step to making a dream a reality. Put your attention on your dreams rather than your dramas.

Many people try to change the world by changing the secondary characters in their story. They try to control everybody around them. How do they do that? It's easy to understand. They love people the way they themselves were loved: they love with conditions. Which means, "I love you if you let me control you. If you do what I want you to do, we can be so happy." We learn to love everybody with conditions, because everybody loves us with conditions.

The problem is that we can't change the secondary characters; we can only change the world by changing the main character of our story—ourselves. The biggest way you can change yourself is by learning to love *yourself* unconditionally.

So, to be clear, you can help me to change the world by changing your own world, through unconditional love for yourself. And when you do, it's like magic, because everyone around you will also change.

People suffer for one reason or another, depending on what their story is. But once they have found a reason, they practice and practice this suffering until it becomes a habit, a habit that is difficult to break. Then, when everything is going well and there is no reason to be suffering, they look for something to make them suffer in order to feel comfortable.

In this way, we can say that humans are addicted to suffering. If everything is okay, we will still find something. It's too good to be true. We have to spoil everything, and then we feel better. It is not easy to break this habit, especially if you're not even aware you are doing it. Even when you have that awareness, you may try to stop suffering, but it is a habit that has taken years and years of practice to develop. The only way to break the habit is to practice the opposite— the habit of seeing everything as beautiful. When you appreciate everything that you see and interact with, your whole world changes. Everything you perceive is beautiful; you understand that it is all a work of art.

When you were born, you didn't have knowledge, yet you learned a whole language by the time you were four or five years old. That was not easy. It took years of practice, as you had to agree with every single word, and every single symbol.

Our language builds our knowledge, and when you look at it this way, you can see the power we have given to the word. But what we forget is that we are the ones who created language—not the other way around. The problem is that knowledge has taken over our minds, and it is so afraid of what it doesn't know that it makes up all of these stories to pretend it knows something that it doesn't. Then we are the ones who feel the fear, but the fear is not real; because in reality there is nothing to fear. When the mind is making up stories and pretending, try this instead. Simply say, "I don't know," and see what happens.

Imagine that you live in a place where there are no mirrors, and that you don't even know what a mirror is. It is beyond your comprehension. You can see everybody, you can see their faces, you can hear them, but you cannot see yourself. If you try to see yourself, you will only see the point of your nose, you will see your hands and your feet, but you will not see your neck, you will not see your ears, you will have no idea what your face looks like. You can see everybody's face but not your own, and vice versa. Others will tell you what they think you look like, and from their opinions you will formulate your own self-image. They might say, "Your eyes are just like your mother's eyes," and "You have your grandpa's ears." You are left to imagine your own face, but you won't know what you look like.

Then, imagine that for the first time you are given a mirror, and you can see your own face. The image

(Continued on next page)

you created about yourself based on other people's opinions will undoubtedly be different than what you see in that mirror. You grew up believing that you looked a certain way, but the reality is that it's not true. You do not look like what you thought you did.

When you find your authentic self, the same thing happens. You realize that who you thought you were—which was based largely on the opinions of others and who they think you should be—isn't who you really are. You don't need a mirror to find your authentic self; you only need to stop trying to be anything, and simply just *be*. You become your authentic self by letting go of who you think you *should* be.

Our individual point of view is changing all the time. For instance, my world when I was nine years old was completely different than when I was thirteen, or seventeen, or when I became a father, or when I became a surgeon, or when I became a shaman. In this way, my world keeps changing all the time, and the same is true for you. Every day, every moment, you change your perception of the world, and it changes constantly as you change. However, there is a part of you that does not change. Can you find that part inside yourself?

"In the beginning there was the Word, the Word was with God, the Word was God, and everything was created by the Word." That passage from the New Testament is extremely beautiful, and we see from the very beginning that the word is the tool the artist uses to create beauty, and of course everything really is beautiful. If we are not aware that something is beautiful, it is only because we are focusing our attention on lies. A lie might say, "This person is old, this one is fat, this one is ugly," and these lies are nothing but distortions of the truth. Because the truth is the only thing that exists, and the truth is that everything is beautiful. Can you see it?

As I grew up everybody told me who Miguel is, everybody told me what Miguel believes, what Miguel eats, and what Miguel does. Everybody had an opinion about Miguel. But everybody was a little different (and sometimes a lot different), so I had to adapt to all those different opinions and create an image that would satisfy everybody. That is how I created the image of Miguel, and I really believed that I was Miguel.

By creating the image of Miguel, I accumulated all the knowledge that my parents taught me, that my school taught me, that my brothers taught me, all of it. I learned from everyone about who I was, but the main thing that I learned from all of them was how to love. This ultimately became the biggest problem, because I learned how to love with conditions. I learned that I would be loved if I played by the rules, if I behaved, and if I loved the way they

(Continued on next page)

wanted me to love. If you're a good boy, Miguel, then I will love you. If not, I will reject you.

We learn that from the society around us, and in turn, that is how we love everybody. We love them if they let us control them. That is how we try to control each other all the time, but believe it or not, this isn't even the worst part. The worst part is that I learned to love myself the same way. I learned to love myself with conditions. The wisdom of the artist is that there is another way, and when we find it, we find our freedom.

The first key to creating heaven on earth is to accept yourself just the way you are right now. Recognize that you are perfect just the way you are, and really believe that you are perfect just the way you are. This is the very first step, and it is not easy. You, and very likely others in your life, have been telling yourself something different for a long, long time. So you have to practice accepting yourself and seeing yourself as perfect, over and over again. This is the first step. Practice, practice, practice. That is what makes you the master. The amazing thing is that as you do this everything starts shifting and changing—and I mean everything.

Whatever assumption you make about anything, and I mean *anything*, is really just a projection of whatever is happening in your own mind. That's all. Look at your beliefs, are they true? How can you know that everything you have learned in your life is true? You can't, you're just making an assumption that it is true. Is that a chair you're sitting in? Are you sure? When you drop all your assumptions and admit that you don't know, a whole new world opens up to you.

I magine you are making a movie, and you are the producer, the director, and the main actor of the story. Obviously no one can change the movie but you. Your life is exactly the same, but it is your movie, your story, and only you can change it. The Toltec agreements are tools to help people change their own stories. These tools are really just psychology in action. You don't need to understand all those academic concepts that have weird names—that's just more knowledge. You only need to understand, first, that the whole story is not real, it is not true, it's just a story. Secondly, whatever happened in the past perhaps was true when it happened, but right now it is not true.

When you understand this, you can understand that your whole past is simply a point of reference for the decisions you can make today. If you decide today to change your life, you don't need all the garbage of

(Continued on next page)

the past. One of the biggest tools you can use is to forgive and forget that past, because it is not true. It's not real. Only what you are doing in the present moment is real and true.

Mitote is a Nahuatl word which means "chaos"—it's as if there were a thousand people talking at the same time in your mind, but nobody's listening. There are so many thoughts with so many different voices that even when you have a very powerful moment or experience in which you see the truth, knowledge will try and convince you that it wasn't real. It is important to be skeptical of the voices within, as well as the ones without. Don't let the voice of knowledge take you away from your truth.

J ust imagine that Planet Earth is like a school where life is the teacher, and life creates all the events that are happening in the world in order to provide lessons to every single human. It's like you are the apprentice and life is the master, but of course you are life, too.

In this way, we can say that life is teaching life, and everything in between is there so that life can have the experience of life. The whole of creation is what is in between life and life. That is the school of the Planet Earth, or what I like to call our *universe-ity*, where life is becoming conscious that it is alive.

The biggest addiction that humans have is an addiction to suffering. As we grow up we see everyone around us suffering—our parents are suffering, our siblings are suffering, everyone around us at school is suffering—and we learn to suffer just like them. We have the best teachers all around us, and practice makes the master. It is from all of our teachers that the main character of our story learned exactly how to suffer, how to judge, how to manipulate, how to punish, and more. Until we wake up, we are not happy if we don't suffer regularly.

The real conflict inside us is the conflict between truth and lies. If we believe in the truth, our mind is calm, and if we believe in lies, we are in turmoil. Anytime you feel jealousy, anger, resentment, or any other negative emotion, then you can be certain you are believing a lie. Our level of internal turmoil depends on how deep the lie goes. The larger the lie, the more we suffer.

The irony is that, despite our suffering, we often become fanatics as we try to defend the lie. We want to believe it so badly. We make it so important that despite the internal conflict it creates in our minds we just cannot let it go.

Wherever we go, we see all these beautiful creations of humans: homes, cars, freeways, buildings, stadiums—whatever we see, we remember that it all first existed in the human mind. We made it real with action. Look at the ancient Egyptians, the Sumerians, the Greeks, the Hindus, and many others, where we see the great civilizations that existed around Planet Earth. We understand that they first existed in the human mind, and then, with actions, people made what they imagined come true. In the same way, you cannot make your own dreams come true without action. Whatever happens in your mind will end in your mind and cannot become real until you take the action. For your dreams to become real, action must follow inspiration.

Where is your attention, your focus? Are you just listening to the voice in your head, or are you perceiving your feelings? What you feel comes from your integrity. Your stories are coming from the "I am not." Your judgment is coming from the "I am not." Your insecurities are coming from the "I am not." But what you feel, without a narrative, is authentic.

You are so used to the message of the "I am not," which has a voice in everybody's head. It's talking all the time. But what is the message of the "I am"?

There are situations where pain cannot be avoided. The body hurts, and you experience pain. Suffering, on the other hand, is optional. You don't have to focus your attention on your pain. If you focus attention on pain, the pain becomes bigger. But as soon as you focus your attention on something else, it is like you are ignoring the pain. Yes, the pain is there, but you are acting on something else that makes you happy. In this way, you begin to understand that pain is happening in your body, but suffering is taking place in your mind.

Can you imagine living your life with unconditional love, without any expectation or obligation? In order to do this, it is extremely important to understand this: *you don't have to try to be you.* Just be, that's it.

If you can live that, you become a master. You don't have to be the main character of your story; you don't have to be the way you see yourself. In fact, you don't have to expect anything from yourself. If you can reach that point, all your problems will fall away, and then you will be able to really live in the moment as the artist that is creating the story, right now and right here.

When you try to control others, or make them act or believe the way you want them to, you are not respecting them. What you are really saying is that you don't think they are good enough, or strong enough, or intelligent enough to make their own choices, and that you need to impose your beliefs on them. Of course, you may think that you are helping them, but it's not true. I'm sure you can think of many instances in your own life when others have done this to you, thinking they were helping you, and that wasn't true either. When you stop trying to push your beliefs and ideas on others, only then are you truly respecting them. You are letting them know that they are good enough, intelligent enough, and strong enough to make their own choices in life. That is being truly helpful. That is real love, and it is based on respect.

On this beautiful Planet Earth we have seven billion people, and we all are artists. It doesn't matter where we were born, or what language we speak, or what religion we have, or what philosophy we follow—we all are artists, each one of us. I'm talking about the totality of humanity around this beautiful Planet Earth. Of course many people are not aware that they are artists, but once you have that awareness and you see that your art is your own story, then it's easy to understand that if you don't like your own story only you can change it. Nobody else can change it, but you can change it. Similarly, you cannot change anybody else's story. You cannot change your beloved's story, your children's story, your parents', or anybody else's.

Humans have been searching for the truth for millennia, and trying to understand truth can look very complicated. However, the kind of truth that you create in your mind is complicated. This is not the real truth. The mind makes everything complicated because it doesn't have the capacity to comprehend the real truth. To fill this void of not understanding, the mind comes up with many complex theories. Yet the real truth existed long before the creation of humanity, and it will exist long after the extinction of humanity. It can't be understood through knowledge, and it doesn't need the validation of the human mind.

Knowledge is the "I am not." Even if you don't want to, you have no choice but to deal with all the messengers of knowledge. Just knowing yourself as "I am" may not be enough to live in a world where most people are messengers of the "I am not." But you have a wonderful tool to deal with them. That tool is knowledge, when you make knowledge your ally. Do you understand?

When you become aware, you take control of your knowledge. This will give you personal power to deal with all the messengers of the "I am not," because you know the language that they speak. These messengers will let you know what they believe. You can listen to them, you can respect them, but you don't have to believe them. Their message has no power over you. They don't have the awareness, but you do. You have already learned to listen to yourself and to respect yourself, without believing yourself. You have become aware. Practice awareness until you are the Master of Awareness. Awareness will keep the "I am" in charge.

The word is the main tool of the artist. *Toltec* means artist, and we are all artists, even if we are not aware that we are artists. Everybody is an artist, and the main way that we create is through the language that we speak. With the word, we give meaning to what we perceive, creating a reality that only exists in our mind. When we understand that, we can understand how important the word is, because it's the tool that we use in order to recreate what already exists, and with the word we make it ours.

The word is so powerful. This is why it is so important not to use the word against yourself.

Truth consists of only two things: the first is life, and the second is death. We don't need to prove that life exists, because we all are alive—our very existence proves that life exists. The second part of the truth is death, because sooner or later the body dies. Every body ultimately dies, but the energy that gives life to the body can never die. In physics we learn that matter can only move if a force moves it, and the force that moves matter is Life itself. Everything in the world of matter is just an interaction between life and death. From the moment of our conception when life incarnates into matter, the very first cells start dividing. Then comes birth, and growing up, and before we know it growing up becomes growing old, so that everything that is born is also moving toward death. But the energy of life is not that way; it was not born and therefore cannot die.

You cannot expect that people will see you the way you really are because they can't—they can only see you the way *they* are. This is why it is pointless to feel victimized, or to cry and suffer, when someone says they don't like you. Their image of you is about them and has nothing to do with you. You can, however, change the way you react, so you don't feel victimized. You can change the habit you have to react a certain way.

When we were born, we were programmed according to the beliefs of our family and our society. We didn't have any knowledge, we didn't know how to speak, we didn't use the word in order to create our reality—we simply lived in the moment. But the human mind is a field, fertile for ideas and opinions, and whatever ideas and opinions are tended will grow there. Once knowledge came in and the story took over, we forgot that we are the artists of our own story. We are the ones who created it, and we are the only ones who can change it.

When we begin to break free of the habits we learned during our domestication, we become warriors. This is when the mind wages a war against itself—against knowledge. Eventually the knowledge that domesticated us becomes our ally and the mind learns to transform and transcend itself. We are remembering who we are. We are Life. We are truth.

Once you master the Toltec agreements, then you begin a new way of life, the way of life as a master of awareness. You no longer believe this theory or that opinion is the truth. Instead you don't really believe anything anymore. You witness everything that happens and you respect everything that happens, because you know it is not about you. What finally happens is the most incredible thing: you respect yourself completely, and when this happens, the war in your mind is over.

Everything is shifting all the time. What is true right now may no longer be true in half an hour. Everything is always shifting. The key is to be willing to shift as fast as life shifts, and life is always changing. Always.

This sounds easy, but in truth most people practice exactly the opposite. They live for the future or regret the past, always trying to control life instead of changing with it. This is an automatic way of being for most people. As you give up the automatic habit of trying to control and instead become willing to shift with life, you become happier and happier.

Please, don't just believe what I say, or what anyone else says (and this includes what you tell yourself). At the same time, learn to listen to everyone. That is the key: learn to listen. When you choose not to believe me, or them, or even yourself, yet you still learn to listen—then you will have the ability to discern what is really true for you.

The image you create of yourself is the part of you that analyzes everything, and that has beliefs. This image creates so many limitations that you become afraid of your own judgment. The judgments and punishments you create are what we call guilt and shame. This is how you deal with yourself. You have created your image and you are trying to live up to your image, but the image isn't you. The definition of freedom is to be yourself, whatever you are, even if you have no idea what you are. Freedom is to be authentic. No one else can give you your freedom.

To become free you have to face your fear and you have to win over your fear. Not just face it, but also win. After you do this comes a time of clarity, because now you see fear as unreal, and it doesn't mean anything to you anymore. You will still have the temptation to be afraid, but you can quickly let go of this because you will remember with clarity that there is nothing to be afraid of.

You can try to use words, sometimes with great effort, to describe something extraordinary that happened to you. You can use knowledge as an expression of art to project the experience that you had. But something interesting happens without you even noticing. When you say those words, it's difficult to stay present, because the words can take you right into that experience again.

Remembering this and staying present are the key to creating a new dream through awareness. The knowledge, the former "I am not," is now an ally and helps keep you in the present moment.

Toltec is not a race or a culture, it is a way of life that recognizes we are the artists of our lives. We are all dream masters. A person who lives in his or her own personal heaven—a person of peace, a person of love—that is a Toltec. Practicing respect is how you recognize perfection. When you respect the human mind, and the choices that everyone makes, then you see that everything is perfect.

You have a powerful memory, so you can remember the most important parts of your story. But look closer, and somewhere in your story you will likely find a big conflict. In the greater story of humanity, there are big conflicts. Many people believe that these conflicts in humanity arise between good and evil, but this is not true. Good and evil are just the repercussions of the real conflict that exists in our minds—the conflict between truth and lies.

Anytime you notice conflict in your mind, you might say that lies are winning. But even this is okay. It is still is a perfect dream. All possible emotions are part of your story, and you are the one who creates the story. If you are suffering, remember to enjoy your suffering, as you are the one who created it.

There's no reason to condemn anybody, because as soon as we do, we believe in a world of good and evil, right and wrong. None of that is true. Things just exist, we live in a universe that is always perfect, and only perfection exists. It is only through knowledge that we judge ourselves for not being perfect. We say things like, "Oh I'm just a human, I'm not perfect." Or, "nobody's perfect." Everyone is perfect all the time, and it's only when knowledge rules our life that we think otherwise.

When you are born, you are completely free, because you are just you. As you grow up, you are still you, but the difference is that, slowly, you stop believing that you are you. You create an image in your mind of what you should be, and you believe that you are that image. You practice for a long time until that image becomes who you think you are. But of course it's not you. This image isn't free, because it always has to keep those opinions and judgments happy. The real you is behind all those images, and the real you is always free. Your image isn't real, and only the real you can be free. Drop the image and become free.

I keep loving and loving wherever I go, because that's what I am. I am love, and because of this I don't need love. The same is true for you, and for everyone, but so many people don't know it. Nobody really needs love, because we *are* love. But if you don't know that you are love, then you will go on searching for love.

The irony is you think you will find love in someone else, but when you feel love, it always comes from you—not from the other person. Love always comes from you, and what makes you happy isn't someone loving you, it is the love coming out of you that makes you happy. This love could be for a person, an animal, a place, an idea, whatever. It really doesn't matter. It is love, and it is you.

Our knowledge wants us to believe that we are all these things we are not. From the point of view of knowledge, if you ask me what I am, I will justify my existence with things like: I am a human, a doctor, a father, an author, but those are all lies, because the truth is I don't know what I am.

The good news is that it is not important for me to know what I am, or to even try to know what I am, because I existed before knowledge existed. Knowledge is my creation, not the other way around. No use of words can describe what I am—even the most esoteric statements like, "I am Life; I am the force that moves matter." I'm still using words, and the truth is there's no way to explain what I am, not even to myself.

We are here to be alive, to enjoy life, to explore life, to be ourselves, and it is beautiful.

Based on desire, you will make many of the choices in your life. Desire can lead you in two different directions: inspiration or obsession. With inspiration, you move toward something you want to create. You are willing to change, to flow with life when new information becomes available. With obsession, you demand that your desire must be fulfilled exactly the way you want it to be fulfilled. If it isn't, you judge yourself for not reaching it.

Channel your desire into an inspiration rather than an obsession, because with inspiration your life becomes blessed as everything becomes extremely easy. You are willing to work hard to fulfill your desire, but you are not attached to the outcome because you know it will always be perfect.

Humans have the awesome capacity to dream, to perceive what is in nature around them, and then to transform whatever they see (first in their mind and then with action) and create something new that didn't exist before. Everything that humans create first exists in the human mind, and with action we make it real. The word is the first tool we use to create, and that is why the impeccability of the word is so important.

The reason the Toltec agreements have become so popular all around the world has nothing to do with belief, and it has nothing to do with religion. It is because these truths come directly from the integrity of the human spirit. Said another way, these agreements are simply common sense. You can read the Toltec agreements in any language, and you will realize that you knew these things already.

Once you begin to practice these agreements, you start unlearning all that you have learned from others. As you start changing your beliefs, you realize that only you know what you need to change. Nobody else knows what is right for you, and only you can change what you don't like about the world you have created.

The whole of Planet Earth is the greatest school, though very few people realize it. We incarnate here, we come into our physical body, and we start learning in this school. We learn through experience, though practice. Life creates all the events that are happening around us. Life speaks to us through other people, so Life is the real master in this school that is the Planet Earth. Then who is the apprentice?

Life is the apprentice—the life inside you, that *is* you. The one that moves your physical body, the one that perceives through your body, the one that has actual reactions to all the events that happen around you. So we might say that Life is teaching life. Energy exchanges in both directions until the moment comes that life realizes Life, and everything else becomes irrelevant. There are no more words because we create the words, and the truth doesn't need a language because it is always there. The truth

(Continued on next page)

has been there since before the creation of humanity, and it will still be there after the extinction of humanity. It doesn't need humanity to believe in it, it just exists. I call this truth Life, and I call it Love.

My message is extremely simple. I want you to be who you really are, to be authentically yourself. Life is so simple, but we complicate it. From the time we're children, and as we grow up, we see others pretending to be something they are not. We model ourselves after them. We hear their opinions and judgments about us and we react—we begin to create an image of ourselves in a certain way based on who they want us to be. This image becomes our identity. At a certain point, we believe that we really *are* that identity, and we start acting according to what we believe we are. This is what we want to project for others, according to the way we want them to perceive us.

This identity is what I call a *mask*, and we wear a different version of it depending on the people we are with. When we are at work, we are a certain way, and when we are at home, we're completely different. Or

(Continued on next page)

when we are with friends we're completely different than we are with strangers. Our identity is especially flexible when we are younger, and it becomes more and more rigid as we grow up, but it's never been the truth of us.

In reality we have two programs. The real program is what we are given at the moment of conception. This is what we really are, and we cannot change it. But then we choose the second program, which is completely unreal—it's a big lie that we learn. We get lost in the second program.

So my message to you is to simply be yourself, not who you think you should be. My message is an invitation to go back to who you really are, and the Toltec teachings are commonsense tools to help you do so.

I often use the analogy of Santa Claus to explain the concept of human domestication, or the system of punishment and reward. In the story of Santa Claus he knows everything—he knows when you are sleeping, when you're awake, he knows what you do and don't do. And you better watch out, because Santa Claus is going to reward the good and punish the bad by leaving or not leaving a present. This is an example of how we domesticate our children, but it really applies everywhere and at any age. It's not just with children, it's with adults too—it happens everywhere all the time. Our whole society is built on it.

When someone yells at you, remember that this person is dealing with whatever he or she is dealing with, and it has nothing to do with you. It isn't personal; it could have been you or somebody else. If you agree with whatever that person is saying to you, then you are taking it personally. If you don't agree, then you can just walk away and continue with your life. The choice is in your agreement. The action of another person is not personal. It is never about you, even when you agree with it.

When you respect everybody else, you respect the way they dream, the story they create, and the world they live in. You know that we all live in our own world, which is our own creation. You create your own reality, and only you know what your reality is. Nobody else can know your reality because it is your creation; it's the story of *your* life, the story of you. That's why we say that every brain, every head, is its own world, and only you know what you have in your world.

If you don't like your creation, nobody can change it but you. You're the only one that can change your world, your creation, because you are the one who created it. When you know this, you also respect yourself.

Early in my training I created something that I call the mirror room. It was a little room in the house where I put mirrors on each of its four walls. The room had no windows, and I would go in there and light one candle, and I would see my image reflected infinitely in all four directions. Of course, I knew that these were just images of myself, but I could see hundreds of thousands of versions of myself in all directions.

When I stayed in the room long enough, I no longer knew if my own body was just one of those images I saw, or if it was the real me. Then I understood that even my body is a virtual reality, because it is also created by light. I thought about humanity, and I saw that this was exactly the same thing. Humanity is a mirror room. Life is at the center and humans are the images in the mirror. The only truth is Life.

Humans create entire languages, and language is a perfect creation that works for its purpose, but at the same time our language (in the form of knowledge) begins to control us. Beliefs arising out of this knowledge are only true by our agreement. When we believe in every agreement we make, and we invest the power of our faith in the agreement that we make, then we are in a virtual reality. We are putting all the power of our faith into something that can change in an instant. The Toltec teachings are tools that can help us change our perspective. Using these tools, we understand that the whole world is our story, and the first step to changing the story is in realizing that it's just a story.

When we go into a relationship, we try to project the best of ourselves. We try to impress the other person, and they try to impress us. But after some time being together, we see things about them we don't like. The question for you is, what do you do now?

Do you say, "My love will change them"? Or, if you are hiding something about yourself, do you say "I will change it?

Can you really change yourself for somebody else? Sure, you can pretend to change, and you can repress yourself, but what price will you pay for that repression? The price is extremely high, because the price is freedom. Are you going to give up your freedom to submit to being something that you don't want to be? Or you will be wise enough to say to the other person, "Okay, let's change these agreements we have between each other. Out of respect for each other, we can make new agreements."

(Continued on next page)

My physical body is the true love of my life. If I can make the love of my life happy, then I can have any type of relationship that I want, based on self-respect. I will not sacrifice myself in the name of love. I will not encourage those close to me to lose their freedom in the name of love.

While our whole story is based on the main character—ourselves—we also create secondary characters that are based on everyone around us. However, what we have in our mind is not who they are, it is only how we perceive them. Everybody else does exactly the same thing that we do, creating their own story. In their stories, of course, they are the main characters and *we* are the secondary character. Because each character can only ever be based on perception, we are completely different in each person's story.

This is completely natural and true in every single human: We are love. We are the creators of love, and there is never a reason not to love. Whatever has happened that makes you want to withhold love, I invite you to remember that it's nothing personal. Whatever happened is really nobody's fault. In that same way you don't blame anybody for what you do, you don't blame anybody for the pain that you feel. Your whole world is your creation, and only you have the power to change it. The way to change it is to bring more love to any situation, not less, because love is exactly what you are.

The only story that you can change is your own. When you try to change everybody else's story, conflict arises. For some people, trying to change other people's story becomes an obsession, and they try and control their beloved, their friends, or their children. In these situations, the person they are trying to control often plays the role of victim, saying, "Look what they're doing to me." By playing the role of victim, this person is also trying to change the behavior of their oppressor.

In this cycle of obsession and victimhood, there is no respect between the parties—there is only conflict. Each party declares themselves right in order to make the other person wrong, and their opinions can become so strong that it can lead to the destruction of the relationship. When you notice that you are trying to control others by either being an oppressor or a victim, in that moment you have a choice. You

(Continued on next page)

can choose to respect their choices and release the desire to change the other. This is a step to changing your own story, as you realize that trying to change anyone else is pointless.

The collective Dream of the Planet is always changing, and it is part of the destiny of humanity that the dream is going to change continuously. It doesn't matter what we do, whether we facilitate change or we resist it, change will always happen. It is happening right now, and all we can do is enjoy the change.

The best way to use the word is by being yourself. Stop pretending to be somebody else, because no matter how hard you try, you can never be anybody else. That is why it is so important to understand every single symbol that you learn, and to use it in the way you want to, to be impeccable with the word. Our happiness depends on how we use the word. Impeccable means "without sin," and a sin in this context is everything we do against ourselves. It has nothing to do with religion. To sin is to go against what we are, and one of the ways we do that is when we try to be someone other than who we really are.

Habits are so difficult to break because we are doing what we already know how to do, and that makes us feel safe. In this way, our habits become automatic. The question is, does the automatic rule your life? In other words, are you doing what you know because it is comfortable, or because you really want to do it? Taking new action can be uncomfortable, and that is why it is difficult, but it's a necessary step if you want to break free from the automatic. Awareness is the first step, because once you really know you are doing something that isn't good for you, or isn't what you desire, then you are far more likely to take new action.

When it comes to understanding the immense power of perception, we must start by remembering that we don't really *see* any objects in the world. We can only see light that is being reflected from every object we perceive. Just like when we look into a mirror, it seems as though everything is inside that mirror—that the mirror is real and full of objects—but this is not true. If we try and touch the objects, we will only touch the surface of the mirror. At the same time, we know everything that is outside that mirror is real, because if we turn around we can touch it, we can weigh it, we can prove that it is real.

So everything you see in the mirror is a virtual reality—a copy of what is outside. What happens in your mind through the process of perception is exactly the same. The only difference between the mirror and your eyes is that behind your eyes is a

(Continued on next page)

brain, and that brain has perceived and assimilated everything in your world. With your learned knowledge, the mind, which is a reflection of the light in the brain, will distort everything. So, like the mirror, you create a reflection of life that the brain perceives. The mind creates all the knowledge that you have, and knowledge creates every one of your thoughts and beliefs, and yet none of these thoughts or beliefs is ultimately true. How can they be? They are based on a copy of what is true, not truth itself.

All the things I talk about are really just the tools of the artist; they are what an artist uses to create a wonderful reality, a masterpiece of art. When I say the life of an artist, please understand that I'm not just talking about a small group of people who used to live in Mexico thousands of years ago called the Toltecs. I'm talking about every single human who has ever lived on Planet Earth. It doesn't matter what language they speak, what religion they follow. None of that is important. The point is that we are all artists, and we use those tools and the tools of the artist to create what is happening in our mind.

People can make millions of promises, but are any of them true? I can promise you that I will live with you forever, but I could die in half an hour. Do you want to believe promises? If you believe promises, then you set yourself up to feel betrayed anytime someone doesn't fulfill that promise. Of course, you likely make promises too. Everyone is promising and promising. I promise you the moon, and the sun, and the stars, and I promise you a rose garden. I promise I will make you happy. But do you really think I can *make* you happy? Do you think that anyone can make you happy? No one can make you happy, nobody. The only one who can make you happy is you.

As you grow up, your society tells you what is beautiful and what is ugly, and ultimately you agree with it. But these are all lies. Who says that a newborn baby, or someone who is close to dying, is ugly—or that our bodies are the most beautiful when we are in our twenties? There are so many different points of view. Can you see that these claims of truth are all just lies?

It's time to wake up, because the lies will not survive the truth. Two thousand years ago, Jesus Christ said the truth will be revealed to you and the truth will set you free. See the truth right now and be free—you don't have to wait any longer.

You only can love others the way you love yourself. If you love yourself with conditions, you will love others with conditions. Likewise, you won't stay with someone who is abusing you (physically or mentally) if you love yourself. It doesn't matter how much you love the person who abuses you, if you really love yourself, you won't stay there. That's because the love and respect you have for yourself won't allow it. This is why the agreements you make with yourself—to be good to yourself, to be kind with yourself, to honor yourself, to respect yourself—those are the most important ones. When you can bring that kind of love to yourself, you can share that with others as well.

When we are born, we have no knowledge. But before long, words capture our attention and we learn a language. We learn about religion, we learn how we are supposed to behave, etc. This is what it means to acquire knowledge.

Once we have knowledge, something extraordinary happens. All of a sudden, when we're just a few years old, knowledge starts speaking in our head in a voice that no one can hear but us. That voice of knowledge makes all kinds of assumptions. It pretends to know many things, but in reality it assumes almost everything.

If we go deeper, we can find the place in between thoughts, in between all this knowledge. When we discover this inner silence, we will see that we can control our thoughts, and that we can create more of that silence inside of us.

Many times I hear people say, "When I get that I will be happy," or "When I accomplish this, then I will be happy." They put so many conditions on themselves in order to be happy, and even if they manage to achieve those conditions, they change them, or add new ones. My question is, why wait? Why not be happy now?

There are people who want to be like Jesus, Buddha, or whichever master they admire. What they don't realize is that they can only be themselves. That is perfection. You are perfect just the way you are. You are unique. There has never been anybody like you. No one is like you now, and nobody will ever be like you. You can only be what you are, even if you don't know what you are. All that is meaningless. You are here, you are alive, and that's what is important.

You could think of a computer as your physical body, and the electricity that powers the computer as the life force that gives your body life. If you unplug the computer, the computer dies. If the life force leaves your body, it dies as well. We could also say that the programs that run the computer are like the ideas and beliefs that run your brain. Those programs are not made of matter—you cannot touch them anywhere—and they only work because electricity powers the computer. You are not the computer (body) or its programs (brain), but you are the life force of electricity that powers both of them. While the computer and its programs will eventually break, malfunction, and be thrown away, the electricity remains unaffected. It never changes. When you understand this metaphor, you can see how secondary and how temporary your body and mind are. They are nothing without the Life force that is you.

Perception is happening all the time; we perceive things outside of ourselves and we call them objects. It is true that those objects really exist, but the objects we see are not the objects that actually exist outside of us. We only see the image of those objects, because light is being reflected from every single object as it is projecting into our eye. Our eye takes that image to the brain, and the brain creates a picture based on what is true. But it's not real, it's virtual. It's just like when you look in a mirror. You already know that everything inside the mirror is only a reflection, that it is not real. If you reach out to touch those objects, you will only touch the surface of the mirror. Your mind works in a similar way: it creates images that are based on the truth, but are not exactly truth. Additionally, there is something else your mind does, because it is full of knowledge, reason, and memory. The mind distorts everything

(Continued on next page)

that you perceive through judgment. You add a story to what you perceive and that story becomes your reality, but in the end it's not true. There is no such thing as a true story.

Conditional love is the cause of all the violence, all the injustice, and all the wars that humanity has ever experienced. When humans love with conditions, they try to control everything around them and try to impose their point of view on others. When we understand that conditional love is the source of all conflict, we can see its influence in ourselves, in our family, in our society, in our country, and in the whole of humanity. When we truly understand this, we can see how wonderful the Dream of the Planet could be if we loved ourselves and loved others unconditionally.

The penalties of domestication dissolve when you don't take things personally, don't make assumptions, always do your best, and are impeccable with your word. You realize that whatever people say is only their point of view and only true for them. The result is that you are free. My freedom is the most important thing to me, and I won't give it away by judging myself or others.

It is important to be aware of the difference between pity and compassion. If we feel pity for someone, that is a lack of respect. We are no longer respecting their right to choose to live as they want to, to create their own dream. With compassion, we respect their choices, and we are ready to help them help themselves, if they ask for it.

If you have pity for others then you will also feel self-pity, and you will believe you cannot make it. When you have compassion for yourself, you understand the difficulties, but you also have faith in yourself. I call this courage. Having courage doesn't mean you won't be afraid; it means that you will face your fear and take action anyway, knowing that whatever the outcome it will be perfect, because you did your best.

When you pity someone, you will offer to do for them what they are afraid to do for themselves. The next time they face that same situation, the person's

(Continued on next page)

fear will be even bigger than before. With compassion, you can still be helpful, perhaps saying to them, "Okay, you can do it, give me your hand, stand up. These are the tools, go and do it, go and face your fear." With compassion you respect their choices and their power, no matter what direction they take. It is their choice, and it has nothing to do with you.

To confront our fear, we first need to understand what fear really is. Fear is an emotion that is extremely important to the human mind, similar to the way pain is for the physical body. Pain is telling your physical body that something is wrong, that you have to do something. Fear is the same. Fear is telling your mind that you are in danger, that you better do something or you may be harmed. This is very helpful when you are hiking in the woods and stumble upon a grizzly bear, because it is that fear in the mind that prompts you to take action. This is a real fear.

But there's another kind of fear, and that fear comes from the knowledge that we learned from our parents, from society, about what is good and what is bad, what is right and what is wrong. We became afraid of being punished, or of not getting a reward. Through knowledge, we create fear that is irrational. We become afraid of what people think about us, or

(Continued on next page)

afraid to be ourselves, or afraid to pursue our dreams. The truth is that these types of fears are the majority of the fears that we deal with in our lives. There are very few bears in the world, but we create a lot of bears in our mind through lies and distortions.

We believe that we are living in an external reality, but in truth all we ever see is inside of our heads. Sure, we can perceive all the objects around us, but each one of us will have a completely different point of view. No two people see things the exact same way.

What is a power object and how does it work? It's anything you put your faith in that represents a belief.

A wedding ring, for example, can be a power object. It symbolizes a contract that you make with yourself and someone else. You've invested faith in it, which means you really believe in whatever it means to you. For you to go against an agreement is difficult, and a power object reminds you of your belief structure. It's a reminder of actions and consequences. Your faith is invested, and if you do something against that, you feel bad. Something tells you that you are wrong if you go against that belief. If your partner goes against it, you feel hurt.

Without awareness, we may maintain many beliefs that go completely against our own truth, and yet we feel we can never break them. If we give them up, we feel ashamed or guilty. Our faith is invested

(Continued on next page)

there, but at any time we can reinvest our faith in the truth of us. We can make new agreements with ourselves and others, showing all our love and respect. With respect, we can change our personal dream.

When you see someone making a choice you don't agree with, you must remember to respect their choice. You are not responsible if they choose to live in hell, because they chose hell, not you. The question is, what do you choose? You can choose heaven, and if you have the desire to live in that heaven, it's going to happen. There is no doubt that it is going to happen. Heaven and hell are both right here and right now, and the choice is up to you.

At its core, knowledge is exactly the same, no matter what culture or society it comes from. Knowledge from Israel, Japan, Egypt, Mexico, or wherever, it's the same. All knowledge is a distortion of what is true. It's pointless to dispute what someone else believes, because their knowledge is only true for them.

Meditation is one of the tools that humans use to stop the mind. There comes a moment, however, when you realize that you no longer need to go into any formal meditation, because you are meditating all the time.

For example, if I were to speak to you right now, I would need to use my body in order to talk to you. My body obeys, and because of this I don't need to think about what I am saying, I just know. What's really happening is that I am being present in the moment, and that's what you are feeling. The language is there simply to hold your attention as we speak mind to mind. But the main connection is the real you with the real me. When we get past the thinking mind, we know we are one. The entirety of creation, everything that exists, all the universes— the whole thing is only one being and it is alive.

When I decided to stop being a medical doctor, the decision created a lot of controversy around me, coming from my friends and my family. "After all these years of effort, what are you going to do with your life now?" they would ask. But I wanted to focus my attention on understanding the human mind. I went deeply into the study of my family's tradition, and the results of this study are the books that I wrote. In truth, they are psychology books, but I don't talk about ego, superego, or any of that. I don't try to explain why the mind works the way it does. What I do in my books is give people the tools they can use to change their own story, their own mind. These are tools to apply—not just theory, but action.

That's what Toltec wisdom really is, psychology in action. All my teachings are about what we can do to improve our own creation, because to me, that is real psychology. It is not about reliving your past so

(Continued on next page)

that you can suffer again and again for whatever you did, and then pay for it all over again. All that does is hook you into your story even more.

My teachings are designed to help you see the story for what it is—a story—and to realize that the story is not the real you. When you understand that you are the artist who created that story, you understand that you have the power to change it.

People often say, "Tell me why! I want to know why!" "Why" is not important. Something is, or it is not. You take it or you leave it, and that is it. There are no right or wrong choices, you make them right or you make them wrong. You can create a new dream by making choices, by making decisions, and taking action with awareness.

Our main problem is that we learn to love ourselves with conditions. You say to yourself, "I will love myself if I can do this or achieve that, and if not, then I don't deserve my own love." You punish yourself by rejecting yourself.

When you do this, you'll hear the voice of the parasite in your mind that says, "I'm not good enough, I'm not strong enough, I'm not intelligent enough, I'm not beautiful enough, I'm never going to make it." As a result, you assume the role of the victim, because you love yourself with conditions.

Conditional love is the exact opposite of real love. Real love is unconditional. You love yourself just the way you are. Then you can also love the story that you create, and you know it is just a story.

Because you have physical pain doesn't necessarily mean you have to be unhappy. Just being alive is enough for me to be happy. I know that many people in the world feel physical pain, and sometimes the way they interact with others changes as a result. They begin blaming others and become full of anger, and they think that nobody understands them because they don't know the pain they are in. The truth is that nothing is personal, and that includes pain. It's nobody's fault; there is nothing to judge and no one to blame. The key, for me, is to see that I can still be happy even with physical pain, and then put all my attention on those areas of happiness. When I do this, the happiness grows.

The word is what makes us an artist, and we use the word in order to create a story about ourselves and everything that we perceive. Because information comes to us from all over, we can say that we are the center of the entire universe. From the center we create a whole story, a whole dream—the dream in which we live our life. Of all the tools we have at our disposal, the word is the most important; how we use the word will dictate how we live our life. We can create a beautiful paradise, or we can create the worst nightmare. Either way it is a masterpiece of art. It is our life and it is our choice.

When you become a real master, you have the awareness that in the Dream of the Planet there is a constant process of attachment and detachment. We constantly attach and detach from people, things, experiences, ideas, etc., in each and every moment. When you attach to something, you identify yourself with something you are not. When you detach, you bring your focus and awareness back on yourself. As a master, you can play with that back and forth, but you also never judge yourself for becoming attached. You practice noticing your attachment so that you can ask yourself whether you want to stay attached, or place your faith and your power back inside yourself. When you are ready to detach, you will do so.

The treatment to heal emotional wounds is the truth, forgiveness, and self-love.

Truth acts like a scalpel that opens the emotional wound. Truth will hurt, of course, but we no longer can deny what is in front of us. Then we need to clean up the pain that the truth exposes, and we clean it up with forgiveness.

We forgive, not because the other person needs to be forgiven, but because we love ourselves so much that we don't want to feel emotional pain every time we see or remember the person. Forgiveness cleans up the emotional wound.

Then we complete the healing with self-love. With self-love, we will stop the spread of any other infection in the same wound, and in time there will be a scar, but it will no longer hurt.

I am truth, just like you are truth, just like every-thing you can see and touch is truth. As soon as it goes into your mind, it is just an idea or an image, and no ideas or images are ultimately true. For instance, I can say I'm a human, even though *human* is just a word; and because we agree on the meaning of the word *human*, we all shake our heads yes. In the same way, I can say that I'm male, that I'm a doctor, that I'm an author, etc. But these are all just words; they don't mean anything. I don't know what I am, and I don't care to know what I am, and that is truth.

There is conflict in the mind until the final judgment day, but the judgment day I refer to is not the same one that religion talks about. What I call the final judgment is the day that you judge yourself for the very last time. Because on this day the war inside your mind is over. Peace begins, and it is the beginning of a brand-new dream that I call the dream of the masters. When you end judgment, you are a master. Just as Jesus did in the desert after facing Satan, or Buddha facing Mara under the bodhi tree, you understand that the entire human race is only one living being. We are only one living being and it does not matter where we were born, or what religion we believe—we are exactly the same.

Everything you see is really an illusion. We are dreaming all the time, and we live in our own story. We exist even without the story and without the physical body. Understanding this will lead you to the ultimate freedom, because you know what you truly are will never die. It is eternal. Your physical body will perish, but there's nothing that can hurt the real you—nothing. You are Life itself.

Anytime you take something personally, including whatever another person did or whatever they said, you make the assumption that it is about you. Taking things personally and making assumptions go hand in hand, and you use them both to assume the role of the victim. Your personal importance becomes so big when you are a victim, because in your story you believe that it's all about you. When you have awareness and you don't take things personally and you don't make assumptions, you find out that you don't need to be a victim, and then you can be free. Nothing anyone does is about you, because they really don't know you anyway, they only know the image of you they have created in their minds.

When people say they know you well, it is not true. They do not know you at all, but in the same way, you don't know them either. You only know what you believe about them. This is true for everyone you know, including your parents, your brothers and sisters, your beloved, your children, and, amazingly, it includes yourself. The image that you have of yourself is just an image, nothing more. It is the way you want to be perceived by others, but it's not true. You pretend to be what you wish to be in front of everyone, even yourself. When this truth arrives in your heart, you find out that everything that you used to believe is not true.

Whatever we do in life always starts with a desire to do something; desire is not good or bad or right or wrong, it is just a simple motivation that we have. If we can understand this, desire can be free to go into different directions.

There are things that you like, and things that you don't like. There are things you do because you want to do them, and things that you do because you have to do them. When you have a desire, you can enjoy it. You can fulfill that desire, or not. It takes an action to fulfill a desire, and you can either take an action or choose not to take an action.

When we meet somebody new, we can hardly wait to get to know them before we begin to tell them our whole story—the story of who we are. We think it is so important, and so real. But when you realize it is just a story, you no longer feel the need to tell everyone about it. You know that everyone else has a story too. All stories are perfect, but they are just stories. The thing that matters the most is the present moment.

The artist, or Toltec, training is not about learning. Rather it is about unlearning. We have to unlearn all those habits that make our lives so difficult. In reality, life is extremely simple, and we are the ones who make it difficult. We are the ones who complicate everything. There are so many examples of how we do this that almost anything can be an example. Just by turning on the TV you can see the suffering we manufacture, and you can understand that suffering is our biggest addiction. Every other human addiction stems from our addiction to suffering.

I am here to share my love, and it gives me a lot of joy to do so. That's what I'm doing right here, sharing my love with all of you. That is my truth. In order to share my love, I use knowledge to communicate, to make you know that there is a way of life based on love.

I love to love. What makes me happy is the love coming out of me. Do you understand that? You could have ten people who love you, or a hundred people who love you, or a thousand people who love you, and their love will not make you happy. What's really going to make you happy is the love that comes out of you—that's what matters.

Fear is really the first obstacle in your path to becoming what you really are, and it is the most powerful one. Until we face our fears and win, fear will keep us trapped. Confronted with this, many people will assume the point of view of the victim, asking "How am I ever going to do it?" Or saying, "It's not possible, I never will reach my goals."

Fear causes you to reject yourself even before anybody else rejects you. From the perspective of the victim, it is difficult to find the courage to face fear. But the moment you realize that fear only exists in your mind—in the story that you've told yourself about the person, the situation, or whatever your mind is afraid of—then you have found your power and you become free.

The truth will set you free. That's all we need to know, really. If we know the truth, we become free.

If someone says, "This is the truth, believe me," then you can be sure it is not truth. Truth cannot be expressed in words. You need to experience it. How are we going to experience the truth? Inspiration. When we are inspired, we bypass knowledge and just know. We don't need to prove, we just *know*. Once you bypass knowledge, you understand that we are the ones who create knowledge. We are the creators of knowledge. Through the creation of knowledge we create an image of the truth, but you always have the awareness that this image is not the truth.

Eventually we realize through our awareness that what we learned growing up—about the world, about life, about ourselves—it's not exactly true. This isn't good or bad, right or wrong; it's just the way it is. A time comes when the brain is mature enough that we start doubting, we start challenging our own beliefs. Only then can we start shifting what we believe, expanding the mind so that everything is possible.

We are born creators, and one of our biggest creations is the language that we speak. We use that language to create a whole story. It could be the most wonderful story or the most dramatic story. It could be heaven or hell, but it's our creation. It's our responsibility and nobody else's. We decide what we see, because it is our world. So when I ask everybody to please help me to change the world, I'm not talking about the Planet Earth. I'm talking about the world that we create in our own head, with our story.

Conditional love is everywhere. It shows in the way we love our parents, the way we love our children. You can see it in the way we love our friends, our sweethearts, and the way we love ourselves. It's evident in the way we love nature, and the way we love God. We love all of them when and if they please us. Conditional love is so normal in our society that we just accept it. Most of us are unaware that this is even a problem. Our commitment to conditional love is the result of thousands of years of practice. Despite this, real love exists. Real love is love without conditions. When you say, "You can do whatever you want and be whoever you want...I'll love you no matter what." That is real love.

Just as you are the main character in your own story, you are also a secondary character in everybody else's story. Embracing this truth will not kill you . . . quite the opposite. Embracing this will allow you to enjoy your life. When you realize everyone has a story in which they are the main character, you understand that you are only a secondary character, and this is a big relief. Their happiness isn't up to you, it's up to them. You understand that it is impossible to change anybody's story—only they themselves can do it.

People have the right to believe what they believe. They are responsible for what they say, what they understand, and what they do. You cannot make anyone else happy, because you don't have that power. You cannot force anyone to change anything. Remember, whatever decision they make in their own story, it's nothing personal. We don't have the right or

(Continued on next page)

the power to control other people—all we can do is respect their right to create their own story.

When we respect this truth, we find peace within ourselves and with everybody else in a wonderful way.

When you resist things, you resist perfection in creation—the perfection that is God. That's why it's important to completely surrender to life. When you surrender to life, you don't need to go to a monastery or an ashram to find God. You will find God in your daily work, in your marriage, in taking care of your children, in simply being alive. That's God, right here, right now.

E ven though I cannot accurately explain who or what I am through knowledge, I still know that I am. I exist and I am alive, and life is eternal. The Angel of Death is really teaching us to be alive, and to live as if this is the last day of our life. We can certainly plan for the future, as long as we remember that whatever we plan may happen or it may not. What exists for certain is this present moment. That's why the main thing to do is to enjoy life the best we can and not to be afraid to die.

You know the word *Toltec* means "artist," so when I talk about Toltecs, I'm really talking about all of humanity, because we all are artists. The biggest art that we humans create is a story—the story of ourselves, the story of our life. This story looks completely real to us, and we create it through the word. This story becomes so important to us that we come to believe it is our whole being. That is why I say, "What we believe, we are."

We accumulate all our knowledge through the word. We give meaning to every single word we use, and we limit our personal power by keeping it dependent on knowledge.

Ultimately you can never change yourself enough to live up to the judgments and opinions of others. It's impossible. There are too many judgments and they are always changing, not to mention that you can never satisfy their image of you. If you continue to try to do so, you will judge yourself for failing, and you will no longer like yourself. If these self-judgments get bad enough, you may even try to escape from yourself by turning to things like alcohol, drugs, shopping, overeating, or whatever makes you forget, because you don't like to be yourself. This is the way accepting the judgments of others will lead to a habit of self-judgment. To break this habit takes unconditional love for yourself. That is my hope and wish for you—that you stop judging yourself and love yourself exactly the way you are. Everything in this world is perfect, and that includes you.

When you see yourself as an artist, you can take responsibility for your creation as an artist. This means you can take the opportunity to change your creation if you want to change it. At the same time, if you don't want to change it, you have every right not to change it, because it is your creation.

In this way, you respect your creation, and this allows you the freedom to respect everybody else's creation. You don't have the right to change anybody else's creation—that is their choice. Living your life as an artist requires practice, of course, and when you practice these Toltec agreements, it completely changes your world.

My mother Sarita learned our family's tradition, our Toltec knowledge, directly from my grandfather. The word *Toltec* means "artist," and part of my mother's art was healing; she became a *curandera*, or faith healer. She healed many, many people, and as I grew up, I saw a lot of miracles. She cured blind people, people with epilepsy, people with heart problems, and of course treated many emotional problems. She was a wonderful example of the power of faith and the importance of noticing where we put our faith. When we take action based on our faith in something, it manifests in the world.

We have a world that is made, in part, by lies. I am talking about our shared world, the world we create. To understand this further, we have to understand what a lie is. A lie is a distortion of the truth. We have distorted everything since we were children, because we perceive with our minds, filtering everything through our knowledge and adding all kinds of judgments and opinions to what we perceive. So when we are asked what is happening in the world, who we are, or why we are here, we have all sorts of answers—but they are all based on our distortions. The only true answer is "I don't know." The only thing we can say with certainty is, "All I know is that I exist."

Anything we say beyond that is a distortion, because in order to explain what the truth is, we need to use words. All the language that we know (and it doesn't matter what language we speak) is

(Continued on next page)

only true to the extent that people agree with the meaning of every letter, every word, every sentence. So it's relative. But the real truth is not relative, so it can never be expressed in words. Words can only distort the truth.

The Toltec agreements are a mirror: they really reflect you to yourself. These simple agreements will challenge all the prior agreements that you have, the ones that have caused all the drama and suffering in your life. For example, you might say to yourself, "I'm not beautiful enough," but is that the truth? Are you not beautiful enough? Or you might say, "I am so stupid," but is that really true? The Toltec agreements will bring the power and the ability to doubt to what you believe, and then your old agreements will begin to crumble. Many people find out that almost everything they believed was not really true. All the negative judgments you have accepted about yourself simply are not true.

There is a movie I love called *A Beautiful Mind*, about a very intelligent man who sees people that don't really exist, or they only exist in his mind. They say he's schizophrenic, but the truth is that everybody does the same thing. They may not see people, but they hear all kinds of voices—voices that nobody can hear but themselves. This what we call the Mitote in the Toltec tradition: a thousand voices talking in your mind all the time. They have their judgments and opinions, all clamoring for your attention.

In the movie, when the man realizes the truth— that these people only exist in his mind—his solution is to not believe them. He has to strengthen his will and discipline, and choose not to listen to them. After a certain amount of time, these three imaginary people become quiet and stay in a corner.

Our choice is really not much different. We hear the voices of judgment and criticism, but once

(Continued on next page)

we know they aren't real, and that we don't have to believe what they say, they don't affect us anymore. Practicing the Toltec agreements helps you doubt the voices in your mind, and when you don't believe their lies, your life becomes extremely easy.

There are only two things we can say that are absolutely true.

One is death, as every single body will die at some point. But we are not these physical bodies.

Second is life, and while we cannot see life, we see the effect of life, in that it is how all physical matter moves.

To deny the existence of life would be to deny our own existence, and it is obvious that life is also truth. Life is the energy that gives power to matter, and in that way Life reflects itself onto matter, creating the world of illusion, a copy of reality, because only Life is real. This copy is what we see in our mind, and it is how we create our story.

Real enlightenment is seeing the truth as it is, seeing humanity as it is, and not denying the things that are happening. There is violence, there's war, there's injustice—all that exists. We don't need to present one image, or perceive only what we want to perceive and deny what we don't want to perceive. Enlightenment is simply seeing the truth, and not being affected by the truth. This means you don't need to judge, to have any opinion, you just accept reality as it is. If you can change something, good. Go ahead and do it. But you need to be wise enough to see what you can really change and what you cannot change.

When you always do your best, the transformation will eventually happen. Remember, the process of transformation is not about adding any more knowledge to your mind (you have enough of that) but rather unlearning all the programming you received growing up. When you unlearn the program, you let go of all the superstitions, all the fanaticism, all the stories, and all the fears. You find that all around the world, people have different ways of believing, and they are all beautiful. It's a beautiful dream. None of these stories are completely true, but they serve a purpose for those who believe them.

My teachings are an invitation to you to let go of your past, to let go of your own superstitions and your own fanaticism, and return to the truth of who you are. Remember that you only have control over yourself and what you believe, no one else. It is time to stop scaring yourself.

One obstacle to personal freedom is power. Power can become a big barrier, a big challenge—especially if you feel powerlessness. Let's say that you followed all the rules that somebody else provided, like the government, the ones with money, or whoever. They put rules in place and you had to follow those rules, and you did so out of fear. In that way, you aspire to be like the ones who make the rules, because you think that the ones who make the rules are powerful.

You can become a big tyrant, using your new power against those who have less power than you. But in this system of thinking, there will always be someone who has more power than you, so you become a puppet for them by being a tyrant to those who have less power.

To avoid the trap of power, you must see that this type of power doesn't mean anything, because it isn't real. When you realize that you don't have power over anyone, then no one has power over you.

Everything that we perceive is a virtual reality that exists only for us. Our brain is so perfect that it creates a wonderful dream, this wonderful story. It creates the story of our life and the entire Dream of the Planet.

So, when I come to you and I ask you very humbly to please help me to change the world, you can now see that I'm not talking about the world of humanity "out there," but *your* personal world, the only one you really can change. No one else can change your creation—only you can change it, because you are the one who created it. You create your story and you live in that story, and if you don't like that story, nobody else can do that for you. You're the only one who can change the story of your life, you're the only one who can change your world.

I believe in angels, because the word *angel* means "messenger"—it has nothing to do with religion. There are seven billion angels on this planet. We humans are messengers, so we are all angels. Here is the proof: since we were young children, we have been receiving messages and sending messages; we're in constant communication all the time, giving and receiving. So the question is, what kind of messenger are you? What is the message you deliver to the people that you say you love? What message do you send to your beloved? To your family? To your children? Remember that children will learn not only from what you say, but from what you do. And they will become a copy of you. So your message to them is in your actions.

As you grew up, you agreed with many of the opinions that people had about you, many of the judgments, and many of the ways they tried to domesticate you. Even when the people who held these opinions were no longer alive, it didn't matter, because you adopted their ideas in your own mind. So you continued to judge yourself whenever you failed to live up to their standards. Of course it is impossible to satisfy this image because it isn't real, it's just a set of ideas. And because you couldn't satisfy this image, you stopped liking yourself. This is a state that many people in the world find themselves in today.

Many people ask me what I am and the real truth is I have no idea what I am, but I know that I am here and I am alive. In order to describe what I am, I have to use knowledge, and knowledge is not exactly true. It is the way we understand each other. I can say I am a human, I am male, I am a medical doctor, I am an author, I am a shaman, I am energy, spirit, light, whatever, but all of these are just words. The truth is that I really don't know what I am, but I am here now. And it's the same with all of you. You think that you know what you are, and you use knowledge to tell yourself what you are, and you make an image of yourself and project yourself in that way. Everybody may believe that this is what you are, but is that really true? Can you really describe the power that you are?

Your whole story is made up of one main character, and everything and everyone else is related to the main character of your story. This main character is what you believe you are, but the truth is you are not what you believe yourself to be. This main character is just a creation of your knowledge, a creation of your mind, and it is not real. I know it looks real, and feels real, but I promise you it is a creation of your mind. Now, this character could be generous and grateful, or it could be angry and selfish. This character creates all the opinions and all the judgments about everything, and it also receives all the judgments and opinions from others. The character is the one who is living in that story. So the question is, do you want to suffer or enjoy the story you have created? That is your decision.

Everybody can do whatever they think is best in this journey of life. They can believe or not believe whatever I say. I will never impose my point of view on anyone. Doing so would take *my* freedom away, and my freedom is so precious that I will not let it go for anything or for anyone in the world.

You know humans are ruled by knowledge, and that's just the way it is right now. That's why, in the Dream of the Planet, we have seemingly endless cycles of action and reaction, action and reaction. In truth it is all in perfect equilibrium, because life is eternal. We cannot destroy life, even if we try.

You don't get respect by asking for it; respect has to be earned. You don't earn it through bravado or acts of power, you earn it by not intimidating others, by not trying to control others, and by not using fear to domesticate others to your point of view. The truth is that the only way to earn respect is to respect everybody else. You will not receive what you are not prepared to give.

In ancient societies like those that thrived in Egypt, Greece, India, Persia, and Mexico, they had what we now call mystery schools. They were more like any university we have today. You know, it is just like if you want to be a medical doctor, you need to study until you understand medicine. You can study to become an engineer, or anything.

So, in a sense, every school is a mystery school. This includes some you have already attended. For example, when you go to elementary school, you know nothing about reading and writing—it's a mystery for you. Same with junior high, or college, or graduate school. New information is a mystery.

You can even go deeper and see that the whole Planet Earth is a mystery school. When you were born, you didn't know exactly where you were going— it was a big mystery. Even today, life is a big mystery. Anytime you think you know, you really don't.

At a certain point in my life, I had the awareness that there is only one being, and it is alive. All creation is only one being—made by billions of universes—and that being is alive. So we can say that everything comes from one place really, which I call Total Power. This Total Power is just potential energy, but as soon as you take action, that power starts transforming, because it's in motion now. It starts shifting, and creation begins—power starts creating matter. *Power in action creates matter.* You can see this all around you if you take a moment to look.

There is a war in your head. At some point in your life you probably believed this war was between good and evil, but the real conflict is between the truth and lies. When you believe lies, the result will be evil in different degrees, depending on how attached you are to your own lies. When you believe in truth, the result is always goodness. You can tell the lies because they are the beliefs that cause you suffering: jealousies, envy, resentments, anger, etc. Lies that take hold when you don't have awareness of the truth, and one way to find the truth is through the Toltec agreements. So when you are suffering, ask yourself what agreement can help you get back to the truth, and when you practice that agreement, the result will be goodness.

The story of our lives is always changing, because we never see the world the same way from moment to moment. In my own case, when I was ten years old I saw the world in a completely different way than I did when I was twenty, or when I had my children, or when I had my car accident. The way you see the world is always changing; it is never the same. It's important to understand that the whole story of your life is just a story, and you are the one who created that story. With this understanding, you can ask yourself, "What do I want my story to look like going forward?"

Human beings are the only animals on earth that domesticate themselves. But in order for you to domesticate yourself, someone else must domesticate you first. The moment you agree with them is the moment you no longer need anybody else to domesticate you, because you can do it yourself. In turn, you will try to domesticate everyone around you the same way, and that is how the problem of domestication grows. The primary tool for domestication is conditional love—"I will love you if you do this." You agree to this, and eventually apply that same statement to yourself.

When you see that the world is virtual and not real, it will help you to enjoy your virtual reality. This will allow you to keep going along with your everyday dream and to make wiser choices, because you know that your story is your creation and it's only true for you. At the same time, you're dealing with millions of people who do exactly the same thing, but most don't have the awareness that this is what they are doing. They really believe that whatever they do is so relevant and is absolutely real, but because you have that awareness, you will not react in the way that everybody expects you to react. When you don't take things personally, you stop reacting with all the drama, because you realize that others are lost in their own dream.

When we learn a language, we are really learn-ing symbols, and we give meaning to those symbols. Knowledge replaces truth when we invest all the power of our faith in the creation of those symbols. Faith is believing something 100 percent, without a doubt. Knowledge takes over our minds when we have complete faith in everything we know.

If we can keep the awareness that everything we know is only true because we agree, then we find out that knowledge is never really true, knowledge is only true for the humans who agree on the mean-ing. The real truth existed long before the creation of human knowledge, and it will exist long after the extinction of humanity. It doesn't need anybody to believe in it.

There is no way to explain the truth. We use language to try to explain the truth, and we can get very close, but the only way to know the truth is to experience the truth.

Life moves entire manifestations, entire creations. This is the big phenomenon that I understood that night in the desert: there is only one being, and it's alive. Life does not die. Because we are Life itself, we existed long before our conception. And we will exist long after this physical body dies, because what we are cannot be destroyed.

Toltec is just a word, that's all. In the Nahuatl language it means "artist." So when I talk about the Toltec wisdom, I am really talking about the wisdom of the artist, and on this beautiful Planet Earth there are seven billion artists. They may not know that they are artists, but every single person creates a masterpiece of art which is the story of their life. They create the main character of their story, they create many secondary characters, and they create all the rules in that story.

In my story, the main character is Miguel Ruiz. Everything in that story is about Miguel—the way Miguel walks, the way Miguel talks, the way Miguel believes, Miguel's opinions, how Miguel perceives everything. Miguel understands or doesn't understand everything, but everything is about Miguel. For a long time I believed that I was Miguel. I could swear with my life that I was Miguel, and so it became my identity. Everyone knew me as Miguel. But like you, I didn't even choose my name—my parents chose my name for me, and as I grew up I agreed with it and I became Miguel. I created that image of Miguel with the help of people that lived around me. Now I know this is not true. I don't know what I am. Miguel is just the main character of the story, and the story is beautiful, like all stories are beautiful.

You really cannot change the planet if you don't change yourself first. Yes, you can change some things, of course, according to your knowledge, according to your beliefs; but this will be the limit of your help, and it won't be lasting change. If you really want to change the world, first you have to change your own world, the one you create. This means you need to find freedom inside of you, instead of looking for it on the outside. On the outside, people will put up barriers and lines to try and stop you from changing, but the biggest barriers are the ones you put up yourself.

When we were born, we had no knowledge, we knew nothing. But as we grew older and tried to make sense of our world, our knowledge grew and grew, until eventually knowledge took control of our minds. Once you defeat knowledge, it doesn't mean that you won't use it any longer. In fact it is just the opposite. Now you will use knowledge, rather than allowing knowledge to use you. This means you will be skeptical about the things you hear from other people, as well as about the voices in your own mind. With awareness, you can discern these things and decide what is true for you. In this way, you control knowledge and knowledge obeys you, rather than the other way around.

As we grow up and our attention gets hooked by others in the Dream of the Planet, we create an identity based on what everybody else thinks about us. We want to please everybody else, but of course it's impossible. Everybody perceives us in a completely different way. We perceive ourselves in different ways. You can see the conflicts that will arise when you try to be what others want you to be. Instead of trying to create an identity, simply let go of all identities. That is what I call being authentic.

For a long time after my heart attack I had pain all the time. The pain was all day long, day after day, and it was okay. Pain is not a reason to suffer. Sure, it could be a great excuse, but it's not really a reason to suffer. Whatever I put my attention on is what's important. So I focused my attention on all the things that I love to do and that I could do. I didn't want to put my attention on the pain, or on everything that I couldn't do. I only focused my attention on the things that I could do, and I took action in that direction.

Then, as soon as my body was a little stronger, I started teaching again. And as my body got a little stronger, I start taking people to Teotihuacan again. I started having a more normal life, against all odds. I was enjoying my life, and it all started with focusing my attention on what I loved to do rather than the pain I was experiencing.

Celebrating love is extremely easy. We were born to love and this is our destiny, because this is what we are. Love is how we create everything. However, when our attention gets hooked on fear, we become afraid to express the love that we really are. I like to say that we are all factories of love without being aware of it.

What makes you happy is love coming out of you, not other people loving you. Just because you love doesn't mean that you have to expect others to love you in return. They don't need to love you, and you don't need their love, because you *are* love. So many people go around the world searching for love, begging for love, because they believe that they don't have love, but it's not true.

Your body is just matter; it cannot move if life's force is not there to move it. The force that is moving your body is the very same Life force that is moving mine. The separation you perceive between your body and my body is not even real. If you notice, your feet are on the floor and my feet are on the floor—we are all connected through the earth. Also, between you and me there is air, and the air you breathe is the same air that I breathe. The sounds you hear are the sounds that I hear. So we are connected; we just don't see the connection. Your body is connected with mine in one or another way, and it is just because of knowledge, that the idea of separation exists.

When you become a master, you will know it. It's like you're looking for something, and you don't know what you're looking for until you find it. Then you find it, and now you're the master.

Start by practicing the tools, as practice makes the master. You practice the tools until they become automatic. You mastered anger and mastered jealousy in the same way—you practiced them for so many years that you reacted automatically with anger or jealousy in certain situations. Now you will practice happiness, the way of life of the artist, and it will become automatic and you will become the master.

When you were born, you had no knowledge. Society had all the knowledge, and society hooked your attention and downloaded everything that you know—your language, your beliefs, everything—and you agreed. As a child, you wanted to be like the adults, so you pretended to be like them. If you remember, when you played at "being an adult" your beautiful smiling face would become extremely serious as you pretended you had all the problems of the adults, because that's what you witnessed and learned from them. Then you grew up and became just like them, so you no longer needed to pretend. This is how you learned to suffer.

In society we often hear about "domestic" problems, which really means that one person wants to domesticate another. Whoever has the most power will impose it on the one who has less power. People are constantly trying to domesticate each other. This is the main problem in society.

We have learned to love in the wrong way. This is the method of domestication. We learned to love with conditions. But this kind of love is the opposite of real love, because it is based on fear. I will love you *if* you let me control you. I will love you *if* you let me domesticate you. If you do whatever I want you to do, we can be so happy. If you dress the way I want you to dress, if you speak the way I want you to speak, if you don't embarrass me, then for sure I will love you.

We also love ourselves conditionally. I will love myself *if* I achieve this. If I don't achieve this, then I will reject myself. Here is the source of all our problems.

People want to believe that there's something— some power—that creates everything that exists. They're right of course, there is, but there is no name for it. I call it Life. Life is the force that moves everything and creates all the matter that you perceive, as well as all the matter that you cannot perceive. There's really only one force. Everything that exists is only one living being, and it is alive. That is why I say, "we are Life," and the intellect will understand it and will turn it into knowledge, but these are still just words. We can call this force God, or we can call it truth, but these are just words.

Whatever you practice is what will manifest in your life. We get all sorts of ideas and opinions growing up, and what we practice is what we master. You can become a master of anger, a master of judgment, a master of jealousy, or you can practice the Toltec agreements. The choice is yours.

Our true master really is Life. Life is making everything happen all around us; every single event that happens around us is being directed by Life. And Life is also inside of us. It is that power, the force that moves every single atom of our body, every single electron, that pushes every tissue. Life is learning from life, the life inside and the life outside. And when you finally master the Toltec agreements, you are aligning with Life. The inside and the outside are in harmony.

The Toltec way of life is nothing but common sense. It's the way of life for an artist. We create a story, which is only true for us and for nobody else, and that story is our art. Even the most miserable life is a masterpiece of art, and if we have awareness, we can change the whole story and make it much better. Nobody can do that but us—we are the only ones that can change the story of our life because we created it. We live that story, and if we don't like that story, only we can change it. We can complicate it or we can make it so easy, so simple. It's all up to us.

If you want to change your world because you aren't happy with your life, remember that you will never change it by trying to change everyone else. It is pointless to try to change your mother, your father, your beloved, your children, or any of the people that you know—they will not change just because you want them to change. The only way you can change your story is by changing the main character of your story, which is you. That is the only way. You change what you believe about yourself, and everything around you starts changing. Just like magic, boom. When this happens, it's not that the things or people around you have changed. What has changed is what you *believe* about them. This all starts with changing what you believe about yourself. Understand this, and you will find the truth that will set you free.

When you understand that we create our own stories, you understand why it is pointless to take anything personally. We live in a world that we create, and everybody around us is a secondary character in our story. This is also true for everyone else—they are the center of the universe that they create, and you are a secondary character. With this awareness, you realize that anything the other person does will come from the perspective of their own story, and it has nothing to do with you. In other words, it's not personal.

My parents called me Miguel—Miguel Angel Ruiz. I agreed with them, and this is how I identify myself wherever I go, but is it really what I am? No, of course not. What I am cannot be expressed with words. The name that you answer to, is that who you really are?

When people ask me, "Miguel, what are you?" I can say things like, "I am a father, I am a surgeon, I am an author," and I can tell you everything about the main character of the story of Miguel Ruiz, but where is the truth in that? The truth is that I have no idea what I am. And when I say I have no idea what I am, it's just like a dog doesn't know it's a dog, a cat doesn't know it's a cat. We call them dogs and cats, but they don't know what they are, and they don't care. And that's the best part—they don't care. They just exist. But we care.

"Oh, I'm a human," we say, "and I am the best of creation." That is silliness.

I always say to people, "Don't believe yourself," and they look at me, confused. I say this because for so many people, the voice in their mind says things like "You're fat, you're ugly, you're stupid," and none of these things are true. You are telling yourself lies.

It's important to stop believing your own voice. Recognize that you have been programmed since birth to like certain things and dislike others, until the voice in your head is overrun by ideas that aren't even your own. You have created a whole belief system based on other people's ideas, and you had no defense against all those concepts or beliefs that were deposited in you as a child. So you begin by no longer believing that voice, the one inside yourself, and then you can find out what is really true for you.

Once you respect yourself, then you have complete peace, because you will respect everyone around you as well. You know that people live in their own dream, and you don't need to disturb those dreams at all. You respect them. You can still deliver your message, and the message is nothing but love. If you understand this, you understand Buddha, Moses, Christ, Krishna, and any other master, because that is exactly what they did.

You create your own story, and you live in that story, and it is so convincing that you do not notice that it is a story you created. In that story you create more people as secondary characters, and that includes every person that you know, as all of them are part of your story. But the most important person in your creation is the main character, and that main character is you. You create the main character of your own story, and the whole story is about you. In my story, the main character is Miguel Ruiz. But it is just a character. It's not real, and it's not true. My whole story is about Miguel Ruiz: how Miguel perceives things, what Miguel thinks about everything he perceives. But this is only his point of view, and that point of view is changing all the time, just as it is in your own story.

With the use of knowledge, which is the language we speak, we distort the truth. We say something is good or bad, right or wrong, and we judge everything, and at that moment truth becomes a lie. There is no such thing as good or bad, or right or wrong—no, these judgments are a distortion, and every single human has an image of the truth that has been distorted through all the opinions they have learned. If we don't become aware of this, our opinions become so strong that they will rule our life, and then all we can see is distortion.

The force that creates our real story is Life itself. Life is the force that moves matter, and the force that moves matter is the real us, because we are Life itself. Of course, this Life force is energy. You can also call it God, if you want to, you can call this truth, but it is energy.

If you remember from your science classes in school, energy cannot be destroyed—only transformed—so we are all transforming all the time. Life is moving matter all the time, and as it does so, it is reflecting itself in matter. That reflection is how we create the story of our life, or the reflection of the truth.

Adog doesn't know it's a dog, and a cat doesn't know it's a cat. We call ourselves humans, but to say human is just an agreement, a convention. Everything the mind knows is a result of agreeing with everybody around us about the meaning of things. Every word is just a symbol, and we agree with the meaning of that symbol to learn a language. It takes a long time, years. I don't know if you have noticed, but you can only think in the language that you speak. You only can dream in the language that you speak, which means that everything we learn is only true because we agree on the meaning, not because it's really true.

We create the main character of our story, and the main character is afraid of the unknown, but Life itself is an unknown. All we can say for sure is that Life is the force that moves matter. We can call it God, or energy—it doesn't matter what we call it. This is what we really are. This energy moves our bodies, it moves the stars, it opens the flowers and makes the earth revolve around the sun.

In the virtual reality that is our mind, the main character is afraid of this unknown force. We have created scary stories about things we don't understand; we believe that they are true. The real truth is there is nothing to be afraid of, ever.

When you have the awareness that you don't know anyone, and that no one really knows you—that everyone is just reacting to the image they have of everyone else, even themselves—you no longer take anything personally. We can say that you now have immunity. As a result, you don't even pretend that you know why they do whatever they do, because that's impossible. Furthermore, you no longer judge them, because you don't know why they do what they do. You just accept them the way they are.

When I'm talking to you right now, I'm really talking to myself, because I am you. I am everyone who is listening to me or who reads the words I write, and that is the reason why I love all of you. What makes me happy is not that you love me, but that I love all of you. Love coming out of me makes this physical body completely happy. It is myself coming out. I put myself into my books, and then whoever reads those books really goes into Miguel's way of life, and into Miguel's life itself, because this is authentic. I am not pretending to be anything. How can I pretend, when I don't even know what I am? I just know *that* I am.

How do you change your world? The first step is to have the awareness that you create your own world, and that because you create your own world, it's your responsibility. Nobody else is responsible for your creation. That is extremely important to understand. You are completely responsible for your own creation. Now, in your creation you have conflict. Most religions, philosophies, and histories say that this conflict is between good and evil—but that's not true. The conflict between good and evil is the result of the real conflict that exists in the human mind: the conflict between the truth and lies. You change your world by believing in truth and taking action based upon this truth.

Beliefs are ideas in our mind, nothing more. Everybody is free to believe whatever they want to believe; I am not here to impose beliefs on anybody. I perceive the whole world only from my point of view, so what I see is true for me, but it's not necessarily true for anyone else. Because I know this, I have no judgment about whoever wants to be rich, and I have no judgment about any politician who wants to control people. I have no judgment for all of that, because if you see it from a higher perspective you see the perfect equilibrium in the world and that everything is perfect. Everything is evolving. When you see yourself as an individual, everything shifts. This is when you can see fear all around you.

We can see the various problems in the world, and it's fine to want to help solve those problems, as long as you remember that they are not your problems. No problem is your problem, so don't take it personally. I am talking about all problems, even the ones that you think *are* yours. They are not. When you remember this you can simply do your best and you know that any outcome is perfect. The outcome isn't up to you.

You could say that we are living in a very interesting time, but of course that is always true, because every single day is very special. How you see the world depends on your personal dream. In other words, you can see it from a very high point of view or from a lower point of view. From one viewpoint, it seems like we live in a time of huge drama, big crises, and that so many things are happening that shouldn't be happening. From a higher point of view, you can see all the beautiful living beings that reside on Planet Earth. Although there are all types of events that are happening all the time, these events cannot effect our true humanity. Everything is beautiful, perfect, and evolving, all the time.

When you stop judging everyone and everything around you, including your parents, your teachers, your government, and God, then you have reached what we call the last judgment. This means it's the last time that you judge yourself. When that happens, the war inside you is over. It is the end of your story, and the beginning of a new world order, a world of peace and joy within you. This is the World of the master.

If you remember the biblical story of Jesus in the desert, where for forty days he faces all the temptations from Satan, you can see that Satan is Jesus' knowledge. On the final day he stops judging himself, and with the last judgment there is no more Satan. Jesus becomes the Christ, which means he becomes the master. He starts sharing whatever he knows with whoever wants to listen to him.

(Continued on next page)

The same idea can be found with Buddha sitting under the bodhi tree, where he faces Mara, another version of Satan. He touches the Earth and he tells Mara, "As Earth is my witness, you are not real. You are just an illusion. You are my reflection." With that, Mara disappears. Siddhartha becomes Buddha, the master.

How did you create the main character of your story? Well, it's very simple really—it started with the opinions of everyone around you. Since you were a child, everyone has told you who you are, what you are, even given you a name. It was a big effort for you to try to please everybody around you: your parents, your family, your friends, and then your teachers. Without realizing it, you fulfilled the expectation of being who and what they told you to be, and that has become your identity.

We could say that Planet Earth is a living being that is always evolving, and humanity is just part of the planet. Humanity is one organ of the Planet Earth, along with the animals, the forests, and the oceans. Every single species is an organ of the Planet Earth. Humanity is made of more than seven billion living beings, and together we are one. With this perspective, we can see the evolution of humanity as part of the evolution of Planet Earth. It is during the times of crisis that humanity changes in order to bring something new into being. After these changes, we can say that we reach another time of stability. This is happening all the time, in cycles, and it is part of the larger growth of the organism that is this beautiful planet.

We don't have any idea what we actually are, but one thing is sure: we are not what we believe we are. The main character of our story is afraid of the unknown. The main character fears everything the mind doesn't know, everything the mind doesn't understand. The main character is especially afraid to die, because the mind doesn't know what death is.

The physical body has been dead since the moment of conception. The body is matter, and it has a beginning and an end, but Life, the force that moves the matter, is immortal and it cannot be destroyed. The biggest mistake we make is to believe that we are our physical body. That is why we are afraid to die.

When we are born, we don't have any knowledge. Knowledge comes later when our parents hook our attention and teach us the sounds that we repeat and ultimately master. At some point in our early development, something spectacular happens: we begin to talk to ourselves. We converse with ourselves in a voice that nobody else hears. We call this thinking. With this thinking, we create a story in our heads, and we begin to make assumptions. But in this process, we lose awareness. We live in our minds rather than experiencing the present moment. In this way, we forget that all the things we see are far more magical than the agreements we've made about them. Magic exists right in front of us, all the time.

Relationships can be so enjoyable, so beautiful, and so wonderful, as long as you remember that whatever begins will sooner or later end. Relationships begin and relationships end. All kinds of relationships, not just romantic ones. Everything that has a beginning will have an end. Everything is impermanent. The only truth is right here and right now, and right here and right now you are with the love of your life: you. Even the relationship you have with your physical body will end—it will be the last thing to go. When your body goes, life is still right here, right now. You are life, and you are eternal.

As we grew up, the truth was distorted according to the opinions of people who lived around us: our parents, our teachers, our religion, and society. As a result, we have spent our lives trying to live up to the opinions of these other people, often doing things that go against our integrity. This is the basis of human domestication, and awareness is the key to ending it. When you understand that other people's opinions are not facts, then you can break free from your own domestication.

When I had the car wreck that changed my life, I saw the whole accident as though it was in slow motion. I saw my unconscious body, and knew the brain was unconscious. I could see that the car was totaled, but my body was completely safe.

When I woke up the next day in the hospital, I couldn't ignore this experience or deny that it ever happened. I now knew that I was not my body. People ask me if it is possible for them to duplicate that experience. Well, it is. When you renounce everything, let go of everything, and completely surrender, then you will be out of your body and you will have the same experience. This is easy to say but extremely difficult to do, because the mind wants to hold on.

Once you know that you are perfect, you invest all your faith in yourself. Every decision you make you trust, because it comes from you and you are the center of your whole universe. If you don't like the way you are living your life, you will make a change. When you know that you are perfect, you will do what is best for you, very naturally. It is so simple and so logical. It's really is just common sense.

You are not responsible for changing the world; it is not your job. It is not your mission in life. In fact it's nobody's mission in life to change the world. Your true mission in life is very important, and that mission is to make yourself happy. It is the only mission you have in life, and it's the same for everybody else. You are not responsible for somebody else's happiness. You are not responsible for the positivity or negativity that is in the world. You are responsible for you. The best thing you can do for the world is to take responsibility for yourself.

Don't believe me, even what I'm teaching you right now, until you test it for yourself. In the same way, don't believe yourself without testing it either—this is just as important. The voices speaking in your mind are the old way, and what they say is based on what you've learned before. That is why I call this the voice of knowledge. Knowledge is always talking to you, and you call it thinking. The voice of knowledge has so many different voices that often contradict each other. Your job is to not believe them without testing what they say. You have simply believed whatever these voices have said for years and years, and now it's time to find out what is true and what isn't.

The most important thing is for you to be happy, to enjoy life, because you live in the world that you create. It's your own dream that is only true for you, not for anybody else. Of course everybody else does exactly the same thing, creating their own world, and each is the center of their own universe. Every single human creates their own universe.

So the whole point of my teachings is to help you change your world, to help you stop judging yourself, to help you unlearn all of the knowledge you received from others, and to help you create a beautiful dream instead.

Now you know the tools. The rest is up to you.

Part Three

Wisdom
Stories

*Editor's note: The following Wisdom Stories
are first-person accounts by don Miguel Ruiz, Jr.*

My Apprenticeship to the Toltec Agreements

I was raised in a family with a rich oral tradition. We are descendants of Toltec Eagle Knights Warriors, and every generation shares the knowledge of our ancestors, through stories and symbols, with the next generation. When I was just a boy, my *abuelita* (grandmother) Sarita was the spiritual head of my family and community. Not only did she share the stories of our ancestors, but she also maintained a temple called Nueva Vida in San Diego, California, where she healed many of her patients as a faith healer and gave lectures and sermons to the community of Barrio Logan every Thursday and Sunday. When she was ninety-seven years old, she was inducted into the

San Diego Women's Hall of Fame for keeping the tradition alive and sharing it with everyone in the community.

Once in a while, she would do special services and ceremonies on a mountain named Madre Grande in Dulzura, California. To her, this place was sacred. To me, it was a playground, and I have many wonderful memories of my family there. My cousins, my brother Jose, and I would roam the area with other kids and explore as much as we could.

We stopped going there as often after Abuelita Sarita got older, so it came as a surprise one day when my father asked my brother Jose and me if we wanted to spend the day at Disneyland or at Madre Grande instead. My brother voted for Madre Grande, and I agreed. I was fourteen years old, and Jose was about eleven years old. Disneyland didn't hold my interest at the time, so this was a nice change. I had missed those days at the mountain with my family, and I wanted to experience it again.

When we arrived, my father took us on a hike around the grounds, exploring like we always had. We began to climb the big boulders, finding a little path that took us near the middle of the hillside. At this point, Jose had taken the lead, with my dad and I following behind. That's when Jose found a cave-like crevice made out of four large boulders. My father went in the cave first to make sure everything was okay, and then he invited us to come in.

We sat down and my father began to tell us our family history—about don Eziquio Macias, my *abuelita's* grandfather, about her father, don Leonardo Macias, about the Toltecs as a culture and as a philosophy, and about a legendary two-headed snake that represents the truth.[1]

"I see it as a power sign that you both wanted to come here," he told us. "It means that it is time to initiate you both into the path of the Toltec. Would you like to be initiated?"

Jose and I looked at each other and then nodded in agreement. We had both looked forward to the day we could learn more about our family's tradition.

"Good," replied my father, and then he took out two leather pouches that he had been carrying inside his backpack, and he gave one to each of us. Inside each pouch was a stick, a red string, a red piece of cloth, a leather string, seven stones (five grey stones, a black stone, and a white stone), and an eagle feather. He asked us to take out all of the contents and to hold them all next to our heart.

"This is your initiation my sons, you are the artists of your lives and you are taking your first steps in a very long journey of self-discovery and love. You will continue to engage the Dream of the Planet for many years, you will

---

[1] The Aztec calendar shows a snake with two heads, symbolizing the creation of the entire universe which is made of Energy and Matter.

both get lost and you will find your way back home, and I will be here for you at every step. Take out the stones and hold them in your left hand. Each one of these stones represents an agreement that you will make as an apprentice."

We did as he instructed, and listened as he explained the meaning of each stone:

The first stone represents the agreement to Be Impeccable With Your Word. For it is your word that creates the dream you live in. How you use it will make you either happy or sad. But if you are impeccable with your word, you will always know love.

The second stone represents the agreement of Not Taking Things Personally. Nothing others do is because of you, which means that you are only responsible for your own actions and your own perception. This is the key to living life with free will.

The third stone represents the agreement of Not Making Assumptions. Always be willing to ask that which you do not know. If you answer with your own story, you might begin to believe an illusion. Always be willing to see life as it is.

The fourth stone represents the agreement of Always Doing Your Best. Your best will always change, but always be willing to take action when life gives you the opportunity to do so.

The fifth stone represents the agreement to Listen But Be Skeptical. This includes what I say to you as well. Don't believe me, but listen. Don't believe yourself, the narrator in your mind, but listen. And don't believe anybody else, but listen. The point, my sons, is to always listen with skepticism. There is an element of truth in every voice you hear, but it is your job to discern what parts are really true for you.

Sixth, this black stone represents Death. Death is our greatest teacher; she gives us everything we have and she will take back everything. So learn to appreciate what you have, and be willing to let it all go once Death comes to collect it.

Seventh, this white one represents Life. Our biggest fear isn't Death, it is Life. Don't be afraid to live, don't be afraid to be yourself, don't be afraid of anything—enjoy everything while it is here, just as you are here.

The stick represents the journey of life, a two-headed snake that represents your journey between two dreams. Please cover the stick and the stones with this red cloth and tighten it with the leather string.

Now grab this feather—this feather represents your freedom, your capability to go in any direction in life because you are as free as the wind, nothing and nobody can hold you, the wind and your wings work in harmony as your mind and heart does. Always remember who you are.

Both my brother and I began to follow my father's instruction as well as we could, and he helped us tie the feather with the red string in order to complete our power object, the symbol of our apprenticeship. As we finished, my father stepped just outside of the cave, and with his back to the sun, we could see his shadow on the floor of the cave. He then held his hands over his head so that his shadow now looked like a snake, with the head of the snake being formed by his hands above his head. Next, he wiggled his fingers in just such a way to imitate the movement of a snake's tongue, and began to move his body side to side in a rhythmic dance. The result was that his shadow now gave the illusion of a slithering snake on the floor with its tongue going in and out.

My brother and I were watching the shadow of the snake slithering on the cave floor, when suddenly the mountainside began to fill with the sound of many rattlesnakes, rattling their tails. My brother and I looked at each other in shock—we could barely believe this was happening.

My father was calm. "The rattlesnakes have accepted your initiation," he said. "You are now apprentices to Life." My dad stepped away briefly, and the rattling ceased as he did so. Jose and I were still trying to make sense of what had just happened. "That was a lot of snakes," I said to my brother. My dad came back into the cave and asked us to lead the way back down. So we walked on the path, with a little more urgency than before, and went down to the clearing where we had left our car.

My father told us as we were driving back down the mountain that he was going to wait until we finished school to really push us. "But, Miguel, in the meantime, you will apprentice with Abuelita Sarita. You will both come to my classes and do your best." I held my power stick until the age of twenty-four, when my father broke it to end my apprenticeship.

The Mirror

In 1988, my father built a mirror room—a windowless room with all four walls covered in mirrors (including behind the entrance door). The room was small, and could hold at most four people. He used it to meditate and do his spiritual work with his students and my *abuelita* Sarita, his teacher of our family's Toltec tradition.

She herself had been working with mirrors for many years with her own students, and she also taught us kids, her grandchildren, to begin to work with mirrors through games. For instance, when we were young, we played a game about blinking. My cousins and I would all take turns gazing into our own eyes in my grandma's dresser mirror. Her bedroom would be dark, and a lit candle illuminated our faces as we looked into our own eyes, trying not to blink. We would giggle and mock each other as we tried our best to hold our own gaze the longest.

We knew that the adults used the mirrors for other spiritual purposes, but we didn't know exactly what those purposes were. So when my father invited me into the mirror room with him for my very first lesson when I was fifteen, I was both excited and nervous, not knowing what to expect.

As we entered the mirror room, I saw that there were pillows, matches, and a single candle in the otherwise empty room. He asked me to sit on one of the pillows in the center of the room, and once I was situated, he lit a candle and closed the door. I saw my reflection in every direction. I looked at my face from many angles, and then began to look for the angles where I was able to see the back of my own head. While I sat in the center of the room, I was able to see an infinite number of my own reflections.

My father sat down behind me, our backs touching as our eyes faced in opposite directions. "The only instruction I am going to give you is to look into your own eyes," he said. "It's okay to blink, but don't turn your gaze away from your own eyes."

The candle flickered and I looked into my eyes. No music, no mantras, no prayers—just the sound of the lit candle and our breaths. I stared into my reflected eyes, and within a few minutes my face began to lose focus and look like a dark patchy blotch. I remembered this happened during the games I played as a child, too, so I didn't think much of it. The image of my face would come back each time I would correct my focus, going back and forth between the blotch and my face.

Then suddenly, something unexpected happened. The image of my face changed in the reflection. It transformed into that of a young man, about my own age, but someone whom I didn't recognize. Naturally I was startled.

"Keep looking," my father said immediately as he heard me gasp and felt me press backward into him. He could also see my reaction in the reflections.

I refocused my gaze, and then the image transformed back into a blotch, and then into my own face again. I breathed a little sigh of relief. Heeding my father's words, I continued to look into my eyes and my face turned back into a blotch again, but as I corrected my focus, instead of seeing my own face, I saw the face of a woman looking back at me. Again I was startled, and pulled back.

"Keep looking," repeated my father.

My mind was racing as it tried to explain what I was seeing. I wondered if this was some sort of an optical illusion caused by the candle, and stories of superstition and magic also entered my mind. But then I remembered something my grandmother had taught me many years earlier. When faced with new situations the mind could not explain, "the more you think, the less you will see," she had said. "Keep your mind from drifting onto other thoughts and it will bring the silence needed so that you can see."

With her words as a reminder, I refocused my gaze on my reflected eyes. The blotch returned without effort, and then many faces began to morph from my reflection. There was an elderly man, a child, another woman, none of whom I recognized. The cycle would stop every time a thought distracted me, and then restart when I found silence again.

As I continued to stare, my normal face returned for a moment, and then it widened, my skin turned a darker shade of brown, and my hair frizzled and expanded. Then both contracted, and then another round of faces began to appear. This continued for what seemed like a long time, until suddenly my vision went black and it was as if the whole room had disappeared, and all I could feel and hear was my own breath.

My father's voice brought me back, the room returned, and I heard him say, "Behind your eyes there is a mirror, it's your brain and the reflection of light is your mind. But what you see there is an image; it is just light bouncing off matter. Your mind tries to process light's information and make sense of it according to your existing knowledge. So, it projects its own meaning and creates a story. Each face you saw is a story, but the mind can quickly change the story of who you are, because it's not real."

"But I saw . . ." I began in protest, wanting to ask him about all the faces I had seen.

"You saw an illusion," he replied. "The purpose of the game is for you to understand that it's all a story that you control. If you do not like the main character, then change the story of the main character of your life. Eventually you will no longer need the story, and you will just enjoy the experience of being you."

Why Are You Paying for Me?

Many years ago, I traveled with my father to New York, where he was giving a lecture on *The Four Agreements*. The organizers of the event had set up a place for us to stay in a very nice hotel for a couple of nights. Coming back from the lecture, we walked into the hotel and noticed that there was an elegant restaurant, and all the clientele of the restaurant were dressed in fine attire. My father turned to me and asked me if I was hungry, and I nodded in the affirmative. So we decided to go upstairs to our rooms and change clothes for dinner, and meet back downstairs in a few minutes. I was hungry, so I got ready quickly and put on a jacket and tie. I went down to the lobby in front of the restaurant to wait for my father. Many people were being seated, all looking very nice, as it was, after all, a fine dining experience.

Then my father walked up, dressed in his pajamas and slippers.

I immediately could tell that my father was about to teach me a lesson, so I knew better than to react outwardly. But at the same time, I internally became full of embarrassment at seeing my father dressed in such a way. I kept as straight a face as I could, trying to be as nonchalant as possible. As we walked toward the hostess, I tried to keep my cool and not give away any part of my self-consciousness or embarrassment about how he was dressed.

"Is there anything wrong?" my father asked.

"Nope!" I replied.

"Good, 'cause I'm starving," he said.

The restaurant did not have any kind of sign in front with a dress code, so the hostess, although I could tell she was bemused at seeing my father in his pajamas, greeted us and asked, "How many for dinner?"

"Two!" remarked my father enthusiastically, once again looking at me to see if my face had betrayed any reaction. As I played it cool, he turned and followed the hostess who was leading us to our table.

We walked through the middle of the restaurant, and I was very much aware of the stares that were aimed at my father and me. My legs felt like salt, and it became really hard to walk those few yards that led down this path, surrounded by heads turning toward us with big smiles. We reached our table, which felt like it was in the center of the room.

My dad asked again, "Is everything alright?"

"Yes."

"Are you sure?"

"Positive," I replied.

At which point he grabbed the menu and began to fumble around the table, looking for something. Finding them, he put his reading glasses on the tip of his nose and began to read the menu. Eyes bulging with the magnification of the lenses and sitting there in his pajamas, he had never looked as ridiculous to me as he did right then. My face finally betrayed me, and I rolled my eyes.

"Is something wrong?" he asked.

"Come on, Dad, this is a nice restaurant in a nice hotel. Look at all the people who are dressed nicely and you are dressed like that. They will think you are a rich eccentric, like Howard Hughes, or that you are a fool with no manners or class."

My dad looked at me for a minute. His face grew serious and I could see the sharpness in his eyes as he replied, "Why are you paying for my actions? Do you have such little respect for me that you have to pay the consequences for what I do? Why aren't you letting me have my own consequences? These are my actions, my choices with their reciprocal consequences. What does this have to do with you?"

I could not reply. He was right; I had assumed responsibility for his actions, for his will, and let his choices speak for me, thus my embarrassment and my mortification were the ways I was punishing myself for his actions. This lesson from my father was reminding me that I only control to the tips of my own fingers, that I only control my own will. But in this case, because I was taking his actions personally, I became responsible in my own mind for the choices and actions he was making.

My father explained that in every situation where I punished myself for another's behavior, I would feel the need to domesticate them to the way I wanted them to behave. He also pointed out that anytime we take the actions of another personally and try and take responsibility for their will, we also are not respecting them, as we think we know better than they do.

He concluded with the following words, "Don't carry the weight of another's choice. You are only responsible for your own will. Learn to respect yourself, and it will teach you to respect everybody else. You cannot give what you do not have."

I sat there in silence, considering what he had just said, while still looking into his eyes. "Thank you, Dad. I understand."

He took off the glasses and said with a smile, "Good! And now we can eat."

This is often how my father teaches, when you least expect it.

Don't Be Afraid to Die

In 2002 my father had a severe heart attack and nearly died. As he would explain to me later, even though he was in very intense pain when he was experiencing the heart attack, he was also excited and happy.

I was very confused by this at first, but my father explained that he saw his own death as a great opportunity to share with each of us how to let go and detach from the body. In other words, he wanted to teach us how to die. He wanted all his apprentices to see it, because then we could all better understand death, and could stop being afraid to die.

When he arrived at the hospital, the doctors put him in the intensive care unit, and these units typically don't allow many visitors, so very few people were allowed in to see him. My brother Jose, who was around twenty-three years old at the time, a few others, and I were the only ones able to go in and see him at first. As Jose entered the room he was full of tears, crying, and saying: "Father, don't die. Please don't die."

This was not the Jose we knew. He had apprenticed with my father for a very long time, and I could tell that my father knew that Jose's mind was controlling him. So he said, "Jose, is this the way you will celebrate the death of your father? Get out of the room, fix yourself, and when you're ready—come back, because I need to talk to you before I go."

Of course Jose was shocked; we all were. He didn't expect his father to say that, but it woke him up. Jose went out of the room and came back a few minutes later very composed, and now he was the Jose that we knew. He came to him and said:

Father, thank you very much and I apologize to you. I see all my selfishness. I see that I would spend the last moments of your life feeling sorry for myself, being so sad because you may die— and you're not even dead yet. So, what I did was shift places, and I imagined that I was the one who was in the bed dying. I went even further than that. I saw myself in the coffin and I saw you crying for me, and I saw you letting go of what you were doing all those years. You didn't want to see anyone, and you just wanted to be alone feeling sorry for yourself. I saw how you were so devastated by my death, and I had just one minute to talk to you, and I came out and told you, "Father, I am fine. I have no pain. I am very happy and I don't want to go back. So please let me go. You are alive. In memory of me, enjoy your life, enjoy every moment of your life. I had my time, I enjoyed it, now you do the same with yourself."

My father said to Jose, "Wow, that is exactly what I wanted to teach you." This was a lesson that resonated with all of us.

Teotihuacan

Although the most well-known of my father's contributions to the world have been through his writings, I believe that the greatest teaching legacy he has given us is the Power Journey to Teotihuacan, Mexico.

Teotihuacan, which in the Nahuatl language means "The Place Where Man Becomes God," is not just an ancient city in central Mexico well known for its pyramids, but it is also a mystery school that offers a road map for the journey of rediscovering your authentic self.

My father has taken me and thousands of others to Teotihuacan for power journeys many times. While every trip has been unique to the needs of the group he was leading, he has always emphasized the importance of becoming aware of our own domestication. He has shown us how we have tortured ourselves by loving ourselves with conditions, which he says is tantamount to creating our own personal hell on earth.

One of the most transformative of these trips occurred for me in 2000. I had recently graduated from college, and because I was no longer engrossed in academic studies, my father wanted to intensify my training in our family's tradition.

To summarize, when we first arrived in Teotihuacan, my father had me focus on my body and my senses, letting go of any shame I felt about my body, and allowing myself to be open to all the tastes, flavors, and textures of how life felt to me. Next he turned the focus to my mind, and I became aware that my sense of self is a projection of the mind, or what he refers to as a mask that I can shed at any time. For example, one way I did this was by letting go of the image my mind had created of what a man "should be."

This mind and body work was powerful in and of itself, but it was during the final ceremony of the journey, which was held on top of the Pyramid of the Sun, that my most transformative moment occurred. My father asked me to guide the ceremony of the Sun for our group, something I had done before. I began the ceremony by tapping into the energy of the Mother, by focusing my intent on my feet and feeling the power of the pyramid below me, and then simultaneously raising my hands toward the Sun to feel the warmth in my hands. The goal of the ceremony is for the two energies to fuse in my heart, as if the Sun were making love with the Earth through me.

I closed my eyes to feel the experience and began to recite a corresponding prayer. But as I spoke, my father walked over and blew smoke into my face from a ceremonial fire he had made using the branches of the sacred copal tree. I had no idea he was going to do this, but as soon as he did so, my perspective shifted radically. Everything I viewed had a bluish hue, and as I looked around at the other pyramids, I could see them breathing. I knew in that moment that everything is alive, and I felt this aliveness deep inside myself. I felt like I could create any miracle, that everything was possible. As I stood on top of the pyramid, I was literally on top of the world. I began to cry at all the beauty I was witnessing, and I could feel the emotions of those people around me. I could feel the trees engaging me, as there was no separation between me and anything else. I felt the profound experience of "I am," where I was completely present in the moment, without any judgment for anything, and I felt the Oneness of everything.

For days after this experience, I stayed in what can only be described as an altered state of consciousness, and everything I did felt like it was being guided by the energy of Teotihuacan. When I hugged a fellow apprentice of my father's, it was as if I could feel myself merge with her. Through only a hug, our breath fell into perfect synch, and I felt like I could let go of everything, including this body. Other teachers separated us, because they could see we were capable of leaving this plane of existence. The separation was painful in a way, because I had never felt that type of powerful unity before. It was in that moment that I learned one can have an orgasmic experience without any physical climax, just the willingness to be present in a bond with life. Ecstasy is transcendence, and I also knew that no drug could ever emulate this feeling.

As this power journey was coming to an end, the group left Teotihuacan and traveled to Oaxaca, Mexico, to visit the ruins at Monte Alban. It was in this final leg of the trip that I began to reengage the Dream of the Planet. Slowly, I was beginning to see myself through the story of my experience rather than to actually experience the "I am." As a result, emotional wounds came back, taboos came back, and I left paradise and returned to my personal dream.

My father noticed me returning to the story of my mind, and he pulled me aside. "Now that you know what is possible, you can find your way back to the truth. You don't need Teotihuacan to do so, as the truth can be found everywhere you are. For as long as you are alive in this body, you will have a mind, which means you are always dreaming. Don't be afraid to dream, but also don't be afraid of the end of the dream. Enjoy it all! You are alive, but your body is already dead. So, there is no need to be afraid of death. Instead, go and conquer the fear of being alive."

At that moment I began my own power journey, and it continues to this very day. Of all the wisdom my father has passed to me, the experience I had of "I am" in Teotihuacan has been the most transformative. This book is a physical record of the legacy of my father's teachings in my life, and I am so grateful to have experienced it all.

About don Miguel Ruiz
and don Miguel Ruiz Jr.

DON MIGUEL RUIZ is the international bestselling author of *The Four Agreements*—which spent over seven years on *The New York Times* bestseller list. He has dedicated his life to sharing the wisdom of the ancient Toltec people through his books, lectures, and journeys to sacred sites around the world. His other books include: *The Mastery of Love, The Voice of Knowledge, The Toltec Art of Life and Death,* and *The Fifth Agreement*, a collaboration with his son don Jose Ruiz.

As don Miguel Ruiz's son, DON MIGUEL RUIZ JR. is a Nagual, a Toltec Master of Transformation and a direct descendant of the Eagle Knight lineage. By combining the wisdom of his family's traditions with the knowledge gained from his own personal journey, he now helps others realize their own path to personal freedom. He is the author of *The Five Levels of Attachment, Living a Life of Awareness,* and *The Mastery of Self—A Toltec Guide to Personal Freedom.*

Connect with them at:
www.miguelruiz.com and *www.miguelruizjr.com*

Hier◯phant publishing

‡ books that inspire your body, mind, and spirit

Hierophant Publishing
8301 Broadway, Suite 219
San Antonio, TX 78209
888-800-4240

www.hierophantpublishing.com